Hungry for God

ARE THE POOR REALLY UNSPIRITUAL?

by Larry E. Myers

Huntington House Publishers

Huntington House Publishers
P.O. Box 53788
Lafayette, Louisiana 70505

Library of Congress Card Catalog Number
94-77740
ISBN 1-56384-075-8

Printed in the U.S.A.

Unless otherwise indicated, all Scripture
quotations are taken from the *New International
Version* of the Bible.

Contents

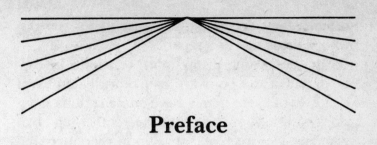

Preface

There are many reasons why I find it very difficult to accept the message that material possessions are the evidence of a spiritual relationship with God, or that God is somewhat ashamed of a person until he or she attains a certain level of material wealth. I have always taken the Bible to mean exactly what it says. Throughout more than thirty years of ministry, I have closed many services with an invitation to the sinner to accept the Lord Jesus Christ as Savior by reading Scripture found in Romans 10:9-11: "If you confess with your mouth, Jesus is Lord, and believe in your heart that God raised him from the dead, you will be saved. For it is with your heart that you believe and are justified, and it is with your mouth that you confess and are saved. As the scripture says, anyone who trusts in him will never be put to shame." I have also assured the new converts that even as we, the Church, rejoiced with them for their salvation, even so the angels of heaven rejoiced with them, quoting Luke 15:7, "I tell you that in the same way there will be more rejoicing in heaven over one sinner who repents than over ninety-nine righteous persons who do not need to repent."

If I am wrong in my interpretation of Scripture, and if the poor are bad representatives of children of God, then I have some serious questions to ask. Assuming that the tenth chapter of Romans is correct, and that upon repenting and accepting Jesus Christ as Lord, one is saved; that the Word of God is true in 1 John 1:9: "If we confess our sins, he is faithful and just and will forgive us our sins, and purify us from all unrighteousness"; and that the angels rejoice over the salvation of each sinner who repents, I have to ask this question: At what economic level will God be willing to recognize the repentant sinner as His own? When will God be willing to say, "This is my son"? For that matter, is there a different economic level in different countries? If the American is judged by the quality of his house and automobile, will the Chinese be judged by the quality of his bicycle or the Mexican by his adobe hut and the burro that he rides to town?

José Gomez lives deep in the mountains of the state of Chiapas, Mexico. José is a Tzolzil Indian; he is also one of our pastors. José is married and has two small children, a boy and a girl. The family lives in a one-room house with a dirt floor. Their bed is made of boards and they have no mattress on which to sleep; José's wife cooks on an open wood fire. José is also presbyter of his area, which consists of thirteen other churches.

Pastor John Miller of the United States and I

went to visit José. Pastor Miller was touched by the humble spirit that he found in José and his family. He wanted to know more about their lifestyle and, particularly, about José's ministry. He was drawing a contrast between the way people live and minister here and the way they live and minister in the United States. Upon learning that Pastor José was not only pastoring a church, but was also overseeing thirteen other churches and pastors, and realizing how rough the mountainous terrain was, Pastor Miller asked José how often was he able to see his pastors. José answered, "I visit each church once a month." Every two months the pastors would meet in José's church for special fellowship and studies. This was all done by foot. No one has an automobile. As we left José's home, John Miller was amazed at what he had seen and heard. He was astonished at the dedication and commitment that he had witnessed in the lives of such a simple people.

Now, my question is to God: "Lord God, are You proud of José Gomez? Are You willing to call him Your son? Are You ashamed to have José cross over these mountains, walking from village to village, testifying in Your name and telling the people that he is a child of God?" I really do not need to ask these questions, because I already know the answer. The Spirit of God has already born witness with my spirit that it is not what a man possesses that makes him important, but it is who possesses the man that makes him important. And, yes, God would be proud to tell the world that José Gomez is His

son, purchased by His blood on Calvary, and that
he has every right to join the righteous around
the world in praying, "Our Father, which art in
heaven, hallowed be thy name."

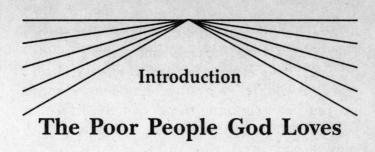

Introduction

The Poor People God Loves

For hours we would sit around an open fire in a small one-room, mud-plastered house. The days were spent working on the construction of our Bible college. Most of the evenings were spent listening to the men talk while the women prepared food for the coming day.

I watched the two women as they shelled the beans they would be cooking for us to eat the next day. After they had finished their shelling, I noticed them pick up every bean that had been dropped on the dirt floor. The men told of hard times that they had passed through, times when food was scarce. Sometimes they would have only salty water to soak their tortillas in, but they were a happy people.

When the time came for sleep I would go to my tent, and they would sleep on the dirt floor of their hut. These people had no beds or mattresses, only a thin sack to spread on the ground as a makeshift pallet. Days turned into weeks; and finally, it was time for me to return to the United States to seek out more financial assistance to continue our work here. As I was preparing to leave early one morning, the ladies asked if they could pray for me. I listened and watched as they prayed. They were praying for my safe travel, and that God would bless my family and me and speed my return to continue the work here. I felt the sincerity of their hearts as the ladies wept and prayed.

Mad Enough to Spit Nails

Soon I would be leaving the state of Chiapas, Mexico, and returning to my home near Dallas, Texas. I had mixed feelings about leaving these dear people. In a very real way I was leaving a part of myself with them—my feelings, my work— but it also felt good to be going home for a few weeks to have time with family and friends. My wife Mary picked me up at the Dallas airport, and we talked as we drove toward home. She was filling me in on all that had happened while I was away, and, at the same time, I was recounting the many things that were accomplished while I was on the mission field. Arriving at my home, I quickly settled back into my easy chair, reached over and picked up the television remote control, flipped on the TV and turned to the religious channel. What I thought was going to be a relaxing evening suddenly turned sour.

It was hard for me to believe what I was hearing. The preacher was saying that if you lived in an old house or drove an old car then you were a poor example of a child of God. He went on to say that our heavenly Father was a king and that as children of a king we should look the part. He

said that the Church must become wealthy because the Bible teaches that no one will listen to
the poor. For a brief moment I felt like Jesus
must have felt when He entered the temple and
saw the multitude desecrating God's holy house
by turning it into a marketplace. For a split second, I wanted to vent my anger on my television
set. At least Jesus was able to take up a whip and
run the money changers from the temple! I had
no whip, and I couldn't reach the man preaching
this garbage; but I am certain of this: whatever it
was flowing through the veins of Christ as He
lashed out that day was now flowing through my
veins. I had just left some of the poorest people
on this planet, and yet some of the most Christ-
like brothers and sisters that I know. I believe
that God is proud to claim them as His children.
In God's eyes, there are no first-class and second-
class citizens of His Kingdom. The blood of Jesus
Christ is the great equalizer.

I've often been asked if the culture shock af-
fected me by going into such a primitive area. My
reply has always been that the real shock is not
going into these areas but, rather, coming back
into the United States. Each time I return, it seems
as though some new twist has been added to the
gospel message. Most of the novel additions are
created to raise money to pay for television time.
The disturbing thing is that not only do such
additions distort and cheapen the gospel; but,
sadly, many young preachers will hear this distor-
tion, repeat it, and ultimately bring devastation
to many trusting individuals and families. The

words of the prophet Jeremiah bear stating again:
"He defended the cause of the poor and the
needy, and so all went well. Is that not what it
means to know me? declares the Lord" (Jer.
22:16).

Was the apostle Paul wrong when he wrote
that "the fruit of the Spirit was love, joy, peace,
patience, kindness, goodness, faithfulness, gentle-
ness and self control" (Gal. 5:22f)? Should he
have written instead that the fruit of the Spirit is
good clothes, nice homes and fancy automobiles?
Or perhaps Jesus should have said, "By this all
men will know that you are my disciples, if you
have many earthly possessions." No, he said it
right the first time: "if you love one another"
(John 13:35).

An experience I had in Mexico will remain
branded on my mind and in my heart, proving to
me that God loves the poor and that He is no
respecter of person. We had made plans to build
a church in the north-central part of Mexico, and
a group of men from a church in the United
States wanted to take a missions trip into Mexico
to work on the project. These brothers in the
Lord had raised half of the money needed to
build a small, concrete block building and I was
going to give the remaining half. The crew would
be able to work for a few days only, so I had
taken the money to Mexico and given it to one of
our pastors with the instructions that he was to
have the walls of the building raised and the
roofing materials purchased and on the job site.
I told the pastor that, in six weeks, the Americans

were to meet us and put the roof on the church. Having given these instructions, I went on to the state of Chiapas to work on our newest Bible school.

Returning from Chiapas six weeks later, I met the Americans and together we drove out to this new mission station to check the progress of the church. You need to understand that where I had just come from and where I was now were completely different in geography and culture. For six weeks I had been in the mountains of the beautiful state of Chiapas, at an elevation of nine thousand feet where the air was cool, and the fresh streams of water cascade down the mountainsides. Now, I was in the middle of the desert with hot air and heat waves bouncing off the desert floor. As far as the eye could see, there was nothing but cactus. The village we would be going to was a two-hour drive across the desert over a dusty, dirt road.

One of our pastors had evangelized this community, and this was my first time to see it. Arriving at the village, I found exactly what I expected: a small dirty community with two to three hundred people scratching out an existence from their adobe houses. There was no electricity or running water. The only water available was from a small pond filled by infrequent rains, shared by people and animals alike. There was very little water in which to bathe and absolutely none to waste. The name of this village was Esperanza, the Spanish word for "hope"; and from the looks of the place, the only thing these people had going for them was their name.

The pastor had done exactly what had been asked of him: the walls were up and the roofing materials purchased and on the site. We worked the rest of the afternoon building trusses, and the next day, returned early and continued to work. Some men worked on the roof, while others built church pews. Our plans were to complete the work at about four o'clock in the afternoon, have a brief dedication service and begin our trip home. We finished the roof on time and joined the congregation inside the small, block building. The women and children sat on the right side of the church, and the men sat on the left. All the pews were full with the exception of the first two on the left side. I sat on the second pew, and an old grey-haired Mexican man sat on the first pew. The pastor rose to begin the service and then it happened. God came.

In a powerful way the Spirit of God entered into a little, block building in the village of Esperanza. I saw the old man in front of me as the presence of the Holy Spirit swept over him, and he began to weep. With his wrinkled hands he wiped away the tears leaving streaks across his dusty, weathered face. I watched as, across the room, the Spirit descended upon the women. One by one they began weeping. It was as if a great fog was sweeping in, moving from one bench to the next until the entire right side of the church was covered with the thickness of the Spirit. Then the Spirit moved across to the left side of the church and, beginning at the back repeated His procedure, pew by pew, to the front of the congregation. Finally the Spirit came to me. I was the last person in the building to experience His touch. I began to weep as I realized that I was in the presence of the Almighty God, Creator of heaven and earth. Then God began to speak to me, and for a while it was like I was completely alone with him. God spoke to my heart, "You have built for me a church and I have come to occupy it." I trembled, I shook, I continued to weep as God continued to speak to my spirit. He said, "You remember when Moses built me the tabernacle. Do you remember when they entered in with the ark of the covenant? My glory filled the tabernacle. You also remember when Solomon built my temple in all its splendor and beauty. Do you remember when they brought in the ark of the covenant? My glory filled the temple. You thought that you were building a church for the poor people; but in truth, you have built a church for me, and the poor will come."

As I continued to weep before God, He continued to speak to me. He said that pregnant mothers would come and their unborn children would hear them worship him. He said that babies would be born and that the pastor would present them to the Lord, that they would grow into teenagers and when they had problems would come to this altar to seek God, and He would be their God. He said that they would marry and have families and they would die and be buried in this church, and He would be their God and would never leave them or forsake them. He said that I had built a church for Him.

That day I realized how important the poor really are in God's eyes.

Does Anyone Hear the Poor?

In the late eighties, I began working with the Indians in the state of Chiapas. In the early days we had four small missions, but we were very thankful for even this small work, because the Chamula Indians had been noted by missionary organizations as being the most closed to the gospel of any people in the Western Hemisphere. These are a people with a terrible history that reflects some of the reason for their closed attitude toward Christianity.

My generation witnessed what has been called the great Holocaust, when Adolf Hitler directed the destruction of more than six million Jews during World War II. Our minds reel as we try to imagine such a wholesale slaughter. Indeed, that was a tragedy that we hope and pray never happens again.

Mexico, too, has known a holocaust. The ancient Indian history of Mexico is filled with paganism and bloodshed. At the dedication of the Pyramid of the Sun in Mexico City, the Aztecs offered twenty thousand human sacrifices in a twenty-four-hour period! But, the ancient bloodshed is nearly insignificant compared to what happened with the European conquest of the land. When the explorers began claiming the new world for Spain, there were over seventeen million Indians living in what is now Mexico. However, within fifty years of the first Spanish footprints on the shores of Mexico, there were less than two million Indians surviving. Fifteen million human beings had died. Many of them perished as a result of the diseases brought by the Europeans, and many more were slaughtered like animals in fierce battles for the control of the land. Hundreds of thousands were put to death in the name of the European's God, Jesus Christ. Their survivors are the full-blooded Indians that fill the jungles of southern Mexico, including the tribe known as Chamula.

These are the most primitive people in Mexico, many of them living a lifestyle unchanged since before the Spanish conquest. Most of them live in the mountains in small villages of only a few hundred inhabitants. Some live in the lowlands of the jungles; most of them never see the larger towns that offer the comforts of running water or electricity. Their homes are usually built out of sticks and mud with grass roofs, and they survive by living off the land. In their simple lifestyle they weave their own cloth and then make their own garments, sometimes taking up to three months to complete a beautiful, bright, multicolored dress. I have reached them by way of horseback, crossing the mountains to share God's Word with them. I have discovered them by boat trips down jungle rivers. I have even had the privilege of visiting with Shamboa, the king of the Mayans in the Lacandona jungle. And, they are hungry for God.

We began with four missions among these spiritually closed people, and four years later we have more than eighty congregations, with pastors overseeing each of them. How is such growth possible? The poor reach the poor. As quickly as a village is evangelized and a congregation established, the young men in their excitement begin evangelizing the next village. In October 1992, we dedicated a small church and ended the service by challenging the congregation to evangelize the next village in their area. We promised to build another church as soon as a new congregation was established. Three months later I received a letter from the new congregation signed by forty-four adults, many of them signing with their fingerprints.

Working with a group of men from Florida, we remained faithful to our promise and built a new building for this young congregation. In only three days the simple structure was completed, and the congregation celebrated its first worship service on the evening of our third workday. We finished the building at five o'clock and at six o'clock the service began! It wasn't forty-four people who came to worship. To our amazement, more than three hundred spiritually hungry people filled that small church. The poor had reached the poor.

Who listens to the poor? Others who are poor; others who know nothing of the "finer things in life"; others who live out their meager existence never comprehending the advances of modern technology. Yes, the poor listen to the poor. And, so does God.

Recognizing God's Grace

Ministry is carried on under the grace of God. A minister's life is often a difficult life, whether that person serves God as a pastor, a missionary, an evangelist, or in some other ministry. So often a pastor will have a vision from God for a church, and almost no one else will understand it or share it. It can be a lonely place, and a place of great sacrifice. Ministers are often blamed for every ill within a congregation; obversely, many receive little praise or recognition when things go well. I said all that to say that I don't believe many people go into the ministry looking at it strictly as a vocation, a job, or a way to make a living. Most church leaders I know responded to a call of God on their lives. They recognized that, in His grace, God was beckoning them to serve Him.

The biblical story of Samson (Judg. 13-16) shows the grace of God upon a called-out man. Samson, born as the result of God's promise to Manoah and his wife, grew into a uniquely graced young man. God called him and prepared him and promised to empower him with the Holy Spirit. The grace of God would be upon him. After preparation, we read, "Then the Spirit of the Lord came upon him in power."

Those chosen by God for ministry are empowered by His grace to serve Him. Even many that eventually fall (like Samson) began under the calling and grace of God, with the power of the Holy Spirit.

I humbly recognize the grace of God that is upon our ministry in Mexico. I recognize that whatever I may be and whatever I may accomplish for the Kingdom of God is simply because of God's grace in my life. One day a Mexican pastor approached me and said, "I know that God has sent you to Mexico." I asked him how he knew this, and he responded: "Because no man could do what you have done unless he had been sent by God." That is one of the greatest compliments I have ever been paid, and I, too, know that all that is accomplished in ministry is done so by the power of God's grace alone.

Recognizing God's Purpose

In any God-ordained ministry, there will be not only the grace of God, but also the purpose of God. God said of Samson's purpose, "he will begin the deliverance of Israel from the hands of the Philistines" (Judg. 13.5). There was a purpose for Samson being born, a purpose for the stirring within him by the Spirit of God. Samson's life was to be dedicated to the fulfilling of this, God's purpose.

Samson was not alone in having a purpose. All believers have a spiritual destiny, a spiritual work that God calls them to accomplish. Paul wrote, "For we are God's workmanship, created in Christ Jesus to do good works, which God prepared in advance for us to do" (Eph. 2:10). Again, the apostle wrote, "And we know that in all things God works for the good of those who love him, who have been called according to his purpose" (Rom. 8:28). Your purpose may not be to pastor a church or to go on the mission field,

but you do have a purpose. We are all called of
God as a spiritual priesthood to work together in
building up His house, His Church, His Kingdom.

I know the purpose of my life. As I reflect
upon my entire life-journey, I see God at work
from the moment of my birth until now. The
time of my birth, the place of my birth, the early
difficult years of my life, my early pastoral years—
all these were preparing me for my specific purpose: to serve God as a missionary to poor, un-
civilized people. My purpose is to take the Gospel
to the lost; to build churches for God; to establish Bible schools and train young preachers and
send them out with the message of salvation; and
to build medical clinics where the sufferings of
the poor can be relieved. O God, may I never
forget my purpose!

As I see ministries rise to the top and then
crumble, I wonder how something so good and
so strong could fail. Is it because of some great
sin? Some great rebellion? Some terrible irrevo-
cable mistake? But, God is a gracious God and
forgiving, and is able to correct our mistakes and
restore our failures. No, ministries fall, I believe,
when they lose sight of their purpose.

I am convinced that one of the reasons for
the new "twists"—the novelties added to the simple
message of the Gospel—is that many have lost
sight of their purpose. They began with a genuine vision from God. Then came the complica-
tions of "modern ministry"—television costs, the
ratings game, the fickleness of the crowd always

wanting something new and exciting. Slowly, almost indiscernible, the original purpose is overshadowed by the need to continue down the path of "ministerial success." Then the abuse comes: wrongfully dividing the Word of God, adding half a verse from here to half a verse from there.

God is calling the Church in America to re-evaluate its purpose. We must return to God's agenda and forsake our own. We must once again begin to pray from our hearts, "Thy kingdom come, thy will be done, on earth as it is in heaven."

Recognizing God's Sensitivity

There came a time in Samson's life when God's glory departed from him. The Bible tells us that one morning after his compromise with Delilah, he rose up from his sleep and said, "I'll go out as before and shake myself free." But, sadly the verse continues, "But he did not know that the Lord had left him" (Judg. 16:20). It is possible for God to lift His anointing off our ministries. It is possible for Him to remove His covering of grace. It is possible for Him to take what was ours and give it to another.

Just look at so many great leaders in the Bible who were unable to complete their tasks because they failed to discern the sensitivity of God:

Moses died in the wilderness instead of taking his people into the promised land.

King Saul lost his kingdom to a young boy with a heart after God.

King David was unable to build God's house because of his warlike spirit.

Israel forfeited the Kingdom of God because of not recognizing her Messiah.

In spite of these shortcomings in His chosen vessels, God's purpose will still be accomplished. He has promised to build His Church. He has promised that one day the kingdoms of this world will become the Kingdom of our God and His Christ. But, let us never assume that God must use us. May we always be aware of His grace, His purpose and His sensitivity.

The Church in America must return to God's purpose while the grace of God is still upon us. God has entrusted to us the privilege and responsibility of taking the good news of Jesus Christ to the world. May it never be said of us that a once great and powerful Church had God's presence lifted from it because it lost sight of His purpose and destiny.

There are three reasons behind the writing of this book. One is to share the marvelous testimony of what God is doing throughout the nation of Mexico. Another is to encourage people who may be going through difficult times, especially young ministers who have a vision from God seemingly shared by few others. The final reason is to help us all come to a better understanding of the value God places on the life of every human being. Perhaps, then, we can return to a balance in our ministries. We can turn our focus away from enormous material prosperity to the prosperity of body, soul and spirit that God desires for His people.

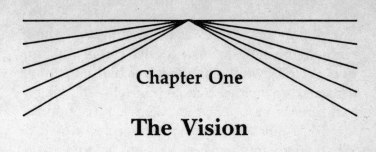

Chapter One

The Vision

The year was 1978, and there was something stirring within me, something both familiar and strange—it was like déjà vu. Had this same thing happened to me before? I was not sure what I was sensing, but I knew that somewhere in the past I had sensed these feelings before. Then I recognized it: after sixteen years of pastoring, God was now going to change my ministry.

The One-Chair Barbershop

The first time I had experienced this unique stirring was in the early 1960s when God first called me into ministry. As I felt that familiar tugging, my mind returned to those early days. It had been so clear cut, so precise. I was a very young man in my early twenties working in my own little one-chair barbershop. One particular Saturday began as normal but didn't stay that way long. Saturdays were the bread and butter days for barbers (by far the busiest day of the week). Often, I would start cutting hair at seven o'clock in the morning and not stop—not even for a break—until seven o'clock in the evening. This Saturday began with the normal busy routine, but by ten o'clock that morning everything seemed to shut down: no cars pulling in, no unexpected customers, no schoolchildren getting trimmed up before Sunday church. Thinking I had time for a brief break, I took this opportunity for a quick moment of prayer and worship. What I had intended to be only a momentary devotion turned into a half-hour prayer time, and those thirty minutes began the birth process for a lifetime of ministry. God was giving me a vision for my life.

As I walked back and forth across the small barbershop, praying aloud to my Maker and Savior, I suddenly started crying as I felt the Spirit of God come upon me. Then, God showed me a vision of multitudes of people standing before me while I preached the gospel to them. I saw hundreds coming forward to accept the Lord Jesus as I gave the invitation. I don't know exactly how long this vision lasted, but I found myself saying, "Yes Lord, I will go. I will preach your Gospel."

The moment I said yes to this call to service— the very moment—the whole world seemed to jump into overdrive. Cars began to pull into the parking lot; and, within minutes, the shop was full. I remained busy the rest of the day, but I knew my haircutting days were limited. I had been called. I had accepted, and soon I would go into full-time ministry.

Called Again

Here I was, sixteen years later, an experienced pastor; and that same strange awareness of God's stirring was coming upon me again. I recognized what was happening: God was calling me to a new ministry. This time there was no vision to see with my eyes; there were no multitudes standing before me; I was not giving an invitation for salvation; nor were there hundreds coming forward. This calling was different. I began sensing a deep desire to take the gospel to a people who didn't have the privilege of a church on every corner. I began to long to take the good news about Jesus to people that had never heard His name. This task would be so much more difficult than anything I had done before. There would be new demands, new hurdles to cross, a new language to learn. But, none of these things daunted me. I had sensed the heart of God.

A Primer on Visions

Receiving a vision for ministry from God can be difficult. It is my observation that He usually gives the vision to only one person. It would seem so helpful if others would have the same experience in calling as the individual. How wonderful if the missionary, his wife, his family, his friends, his supporters—in short, everyone who touches his life—were to all share the same passionate vision from the heart of God. Yet, it seems that God speaks to a single person at first, and that person marries his faith to the vision like two links in a chain. From there the vision begins to grow as others join their faith together to create a network of ministry that will fulfill God's plan.

How was I going to announce my departure to the congregation I now served? I had pioneered the church ten years earlier. We had gone through

two building programs together. We had grown
from ten to nearly three hundred. How was I
going to tell my wife that we would be giving up
our pastorate and heading to the mission field?
How would I tell my two sons? My parents? My
friends?

Moses must have felt like this that day he saw
God in the burning bush: "The Lord said, 'I have
indeed seen the misery of my people in Egypt. I
have heard them crying out because of their slave
drivers, and I am concerned about their sufferings. . . . So now, go. I am sending you to Pharaoh to bring my people the Israelites out of
Egypt'" (Exod. 3:7-10).

But Moses said to God, "Who am I, that I
should go to Pharaoh and bring the Israelites out
of Egypt. . . . What if they do not believe or listen
to me . . . ?" (Exod. 3:11; 4:1).

Moses was concerned about his credibility.
What if the Egyptians didn't heed him? What if
his own people scoffed? But, long before encoun-
tering either the Egyptians or the people of Israel, there would be others that would have to
believe in him. There was Zipporah, Moses' wife.
How would she take the news that they would be
leaving familiar surroundings and going before
Pharaoh to plead the cause of the Israelites? He
could hear her now, "Moses, you've been in the
sun too long!" Oh, if only she had been there to
see the burning bush and hear the voice of God!
If only she had shared in that vision. But, no; she
would have to trust her husband. One man and
one man alone had seen the vision. One man and

one man alone had been called of God to free Israel. But, one man with God's grace can make the difference.

There would be others for Moses to convince: Jethro, his father-in-law (who later became a wise counselor for him); Aaron, his brother (who would become his spokesman); Joshua and Caleb; and all the leaders. Oh, that they could have been there that day as God spoke from the bush.

Because they had not seen the vision or heard the voice, even those who believed Moses would occasionally doubt. I'm sure that many times Moses himself asked God, "Why?" Life would have been so much easier living in the desert, raising his family and tending his sheep. But, that was not his purpose.

I remember thinking these very thoughts. I remember the emotional upheaval caused by seeing God's purpose in my life. My memory races back to some of those early trips into Mexico. One time, in the north central part of Mexico, I visited a small desert village separated from the main highway by ten miles of bumpy dirt road. As I was leaving the village I felt the tire going flat (not an unusual occurrence, because times were tough, money was scarce, and tires were slick); but when I stepped out of the car I discovered not one flat tire, but two. I changed one tire with the spare and began walking back to the village with the other on my shoulder. Fortunately, someone passed by and gave me a ride into town. I had the flat repaired and began rolling it back down the dirt road in the direction of my vehicle.

The sun was going down and the night was settling in, and with the darkness came loneliness. I thought of my family, probably sitting around the supper table about now. Then, I began to question myself and God: "Why am I here? Why don't I have the finances to buy decent tires? God, do you really want me to be a missionary or is this just a fantasy of mine?" In moments like these, the visionary must remember the vision—the burning bush must burn again in our minds, and the voice of God must be heard again: "I am sending you."

For every moment of questioning there were several remembrances of why I was doing what I was doing: memories of God's hand touching the lives of people in Mexico; memories of the sacrifices these dear people make; and memories of the sad conditions so many of them live under. Even when there was little money and much need, both at home and in the field, these memories sustained the vision. I am reminded of a visit with an elderly couple who lived in a one-room house that the husband had built of rough saw-mill slats. Slats are the outer cuts off a log that is "squared" in order to make boards. These scrap pieces are always irregular in thickness and width and are impossible to use in building anything close to being weatherproof. I had gone into this slat-built home to pray for the husband who was dying of cancer; and, as I stood in their home, I felt a great sorrow for this poor family. There were cracks in the walls wide enough for me to stick my hand through. In the summer, the hot dusty wind would blow through the walls, and, in the winter, the freezing cold would invade whatever warmth these people had.

The elderly man lay on a small bed in the corner of the room, his wife standing nearby. I knelt beside the man's bed and prayed desperately that God would heal him. A few days later I made a return visit and found that the man was not home. When I asked the wife where her husband was, she told me he had taken their herd of goats and gone to the mountains. Confused not only as to how—but also why—a man so sick with cancer would do a thing like this, I asked her the reason. She told me that the small watering pond that supplied water for both the people of the village and their herds of goats was very low and in danger of going dry before the rains would fall. In order to preserve what little water there was, someone would have to leave the village with their goats, go in search of water and remain there until the rains fell. Her husband felt that the younger men should stay at home with their families, and, that since all his family was grown, he was the reasonable one to leave.

Some months later my friend died, but I visited the widow many times in the years to come. I will always remember listening to this elderly woman pray and give thanks to God for her many blessings! Living in a house that by most standards would not qualify to be called a barn, and having lost her husband to a painful disease, she had not lost her faith in her Christ. She still found thanksgiving and praise in her heart.

My sacrifices, my suffering, my lack—what were they compared with the great need in lives of people such as this family? And what reward for all my sacrifice when an old lady—who had lost what little she had—could still give glory to God for her rich gift of salvation in His name!

Later, I would learn more about the visions and callings of God. I would learn that He does not call us and send us only to see us fail. I would learn that before He calls, He prepares. And, I would learn that the preparation often preceded the sending by many years.

Prepared for Sending

In my particular case, God had to prepare me for the mission field by making me, if not comfortable with, at least accustomed to sleeping in remote villages, eating primitive food, and drinking dirty water. Are there schools that teach survival for the mission field? Indeed, the school of life was God's way of making me ready. In retrospect I see His hand upon me, preparing me from the earliest days of boyhood.

I came into this world on 30 July 1937 just a few years after the Great Depression. Born into a poor family in south Louisiana, I was the fifth of ten children. My father was a commercial fisherman on the Atchafalaya River, working trout lines and nets from a flat-bottom jon boat. Actually, there were two boats in the family business: a small one for fishing the trout lines and a larger one for nets. One of my earliest memories was when Dad put all of the family and all of our belongings into these two boats and headed down the Atchafalaya River in search of a place to live.

After traveling many miles down the river, my father found a place that struck his fancy. We landed the boats and pitched a floorless tent near an ash tree along the bank of the river, and that was the first home I remember living in. Later, we would cut cypress trees and make shingles out of the cypress logs to build my first house. This was truly "the boondocks"! There were no roads, no electricity, not even stores nearby from which to buy groceries.

We would keep our fish in liveboxes, which were actually wooden boxes made of cypress boards. These would float with the top just about water level, and each box had a lid that we could shut to keep the fish from jumping out. Twice a week, a large boat would come up the river and buy our fish. This boat would also carry the basic needs of the river people, such as cooking lard, flour, sugar, and salt. There wasn't much money changing hands—we would trade our fish for the things we needed. Apart from the things we bartered from the boat store, we supplied our family by living off the land. There was always plenty of wild game and fish to eat, so we fared well. And, there was all the water in the river to quench our thirst! This wasn't so bad in the late summer and early fall when the river was low and not too forceful: the water was clear and tasted just fine. But, during the spring of the year when the river would rise, it was quite a different story: the water would stir the riverbed and turn muddy. In fact, we would take a bucket of river water to the house; and, by the time we drank it all, the mud would have settled in the bottom of the bucket. Sometimes, there was a quarter-inch of pure mud. Little did I know that, even at this young age, God was preparing me for the mission field.

To fight away mosquitoes, dad would make a fire in an old pan and then put green leaves or grass on the fire to make a smoke. He would carry this pan into the house just before we would go to bed, chasing out the mosquitoes while we all choked and sputtered. The house would be bug free for an hour or so; but, by the middle of the night, the invasion would begin again. Sleeping four to each bed, we were something of a buffet line for the visiting insects! But, we survived; and now I see how God was preparing me for the many nights I would later spend in Mexico in very similar circumstances.

A few years later we moved even farther down the river and once again built a house. This time we were just a little bit closer to civilization; we still lived on the river and still fished for a living, but now we were within walking distance of a gravel road. Here, a school bus would stop, and we could ride ten miles to a school. Almost every year in the springtime, the river would rise and enter our house. We wouldn't budge until the river was only a few feet from the house; then, we would load all of our belongings in our boat and head for the levee. We would rent a farmhouse for a few weeks until the water fell and then move right back into our house. I remember many times paddling our small boat through one window of the house and out the other. Looking back now, we would say those were tough times. There were no doctors to run to every time someone was sick. My dad made homemade medicines; and, to this day, I do believe that some were better than many of our modern pharmaceuticals.

As a young boy, I would often walk along the river and wonder what life held for me. What would I do? Where would I work? Would I be a fisherman like my father and grandfather, or would I leave the river? I remember seeing the tugboats coming down the river and wondering if I would someday be a deck-hand or maybe even a riverboat pilot. I would see the old paddle wheel boats and wonder what life must be like in the great cities of their origins. Would I ever see those cities? Many afternoons were spent pondering these questions.

We were not a religious family, although I do remember going to church from time to time. All of our extended family were "river people"; and, when we headed up the river to visit relatives, we would sometimes visit a church with them. I so enjoyed those family excursions. I had a slingshot made of red inner tube rubber; and, if I do say so myself, I was pretty good with it. Before leaving on the long river trips, I would go over to the gravel road and pick up a small sack of good rocks to serve as ammunition. Everything that floated down the river was fair game for my weapon of choice!

On one trip the rudder of our boat got stuck
in the top of a submerged tree trunk. The limbs
had long since broken off and floated away, but
the trunk of the tree was still intact. We couldn't
go forward or backward, and my dad did his best
to get the boat off the tree trunk, but to no avail.
Someone would have to dive into the river, swim
to the bank, walk several miles to one of our
uncles and see if he could come in another boat
to pull us off the tree. That task fell to my oldest
brother, so into the river he went. I don't know
how long we waited, but it seemed like half a day.
Finally, they arrived and pulled us off the tree,
and we journeyed on.

Those family outings that did involve a visit to
a riverside church had more impact on my life
than I realized. In later years, the knowledge
gained from those infrequent encounters would
prove vital to my salvation.

Some Things I Learned

One thing I learned as a child was that there
is no disgrace in being poor and that, oftentimes,
the poor among us are the happiest among us. I
remember the wonderful times we had sitting
around the kitchen table—oh, the kitchen table:
let me describe it for you. We didn't purchase
this table at Neiman-Marcus, not even at Sears
and Roebuck. My father actually caught it floating down the river. You see, our table was made
out of a large signboard. There is no telling how
far it had floated or where it had come from. The
Mississippi River in those days would overflow

into the Atchafalaya during the springtime when the rivers were full. That old sign could have floated down all the way from St. Louis! Anyway, Dad used it to build a table that the entire family could sit around at one time, and it was around that signboard that we had many wonderful meals of wild game followed by family fellowship as we talked into the night.

I also learned to share as a child. Living in a family as large as ours, everything belongs to everybody; and there is no room for a greedy spirit. Many times my dad would come in after running the lines and he would have a few pieces of fruit that some deck-hand passing by on a tugboat had thrown to him. Dad never would eat the fruit but would always bring it home to us. There, he would have the task of dividing three or four oranges among eight or ten kids. We certainly never experienced stomach pains because of overeating! On one occasion someone had thrown grapefruit to my father. None of us had ever seen one, and we thought they were over-sized oranges. They were the most bitter oranges we had ever tasted! We tried salt and sugar, but nothing helped cut the sour flavor.

One day we looked toward the river and saw Dad trying to herd a flock of tame geese toward the house. We all ran out and helped corral them into a little wire pen. We didn't know where they had come from, but it was springtime and the river was high and these geese just came floating by. My dad took this as an unexpected blessing—sent word up the river to my uncle and his large family—and prepared a feast for us all that extended for several days, until the geese were all gone.

Another lesson learned in childhood was responsibility. We knew what it meant to be depended on. When I was about eleven years old, my entire family came down with the flu. Everyone was sick in bed except me. Mom, dad, brothers and sisters were under the weather, and I had to care for them all. I would go outside and cut the wood to build a fire in the stove and cook for the family (mind you, at eleven years of age). I also had to keep wood in the wood-burning heater to drive away the cold chill of winter. It wasn't a matter of whether I liked what I was doing or whether I wanted to do it; it simply had to be done. I had a responsibility. I learned that, regardless of how difficult the situation, there is always a solution—always a way to get the job done. This would be of much value to me later as I faced so many difficulties and shortages in Mexico. Improvisation is a spiritual gift on the mission field.

By the time I was twelve years old I was helping the family, not only with woodcutting and fishing chores, but also by providing wild game for the table. This was my favorite "duty." Dad had an old singleshot, twelve-gauge shotgun that came apart into three pieces each time it was fired. After each shot, I would try to grab hold of the fore-arm, the stock and the barrel to keep them from falling to the ground. I hunted everything with that old gun: ducks, rabbits, squirrels

and every type of bird found in south Louisiana.
I guess it's true when they say Cajuns will eat
almost anything. It didn't matter what I brought
in; my mom had a way of making it taste heavenly. She always cooked everything with gravy
and made rice to go with it. With twelve mouths
to feed, rice was the most economical way to
stretch a meal. Mom always used lots of onions,
and the quality (not the quantity) of gravy depended on the amount of meat that we would
furnish. Sometimes it was rich and thick and good,
and sometimes it was what we called "a long, thin
gravy." One day, times were so tough that Mom
sent me to the nearest store, two miles from home,
to buy a dime's worth of beans and a dime's
worth of rice and a nickel's worth of salt meat.
With that, she was able to prepare a meal for her
family.

Hunting was not the only thing I did to help
the family. I picked cotton during the summer
and fished the rest of the year. I can remember
picking on the same cotton row with my mom.
From a twenty-five-pound flour sack, she made a
small cotton sack for me which I would cram
until full and then dump into her larger sack. She
made shirts from the same flour sacks. My class-
mates would tell me they knew that I was wearing
a flour sack shirt because their mother had bought
a sack of flour that looked just like my shirt.

Picking cotton was hard work, but fishing was
fun. When my older brothers joined the army
and went to Korea, I was left with the responsibility of helping Dad make the living. I was told

that, as the oldest son still at home, I would have to help my father raise the long hoop nets. He could fish the trout lines alone, but one man just couldn't raise the nets. That meant that I would have to miss two days of school every week. The principal said it would be impossible for me to miss that much school, so I told him that my only recourse was to quit. He had a change of heart and gave me permission to miss with the stipulation that I had to maintain good grades. For the duration of my education I missed every Monday and Friday, spending those days on the river with my father.

My high school graduation was a privilege, and a first for my family. Three days later I enlisted in the United States Air Force. In the 1950s, it was common for young servicemen to allot a portion of their paycheck to be returned to their families. The government actually encouraged this action by matching the amount sent home in an effort to help the nation's families recover from a hard depression followed by a world war. My base pay was eighty dollars a month, and I sent half of this home. This meant a total of eighty dollars was going to my parents every month. Of the remaining forty, I usually sent another twenty dollars home in the form of a personal money order, and I survived on the remaining twenty. This continued for two years, until I met and married my wife.

I did not realize at this time that this, too, was part of my preparation for the mission field. As I said earlier, God does not send us until He has prepared us. The mission field would call for the greatest sacrifices of my life—I would be sacrificing time with my family, finances, energy; and, on several occasions, even my life was held in the balance. But, I was prepared for this through a unique childhood and a military service that made my needy family a priority.

I had only been in the service a few months when I came to know Jesus Christ as Lord and Savior. One night, I returned to my room in the barracks at Lackland Air Force Base in San Antonio, Texas. Retiring to bed for the evening, I was suddenly aware that God was speaking to me. How strange! How unexpected—that someone like me with no spiritual upbringing would suddenly find myself in communication with the Creator and Redeemer of all. No one had witnessed to me. I hadn't been to church. I hadn't been meditating on spiritual things. But, as I lay on the bed, I began to pray and soon found myself on my knees weeping and inviting Christ into my life. I started going to the base chapel and began to grow in both the grace and knowledge of our Lord. A few months later I was transferred to Perrin Field in Denison, Texas, and began attending a little Assembly of God church. It was there that I first met the love of my life. Only a short time later, on 25 May 1957, Mary Lou Ross became Mrs. Larry Myers.

This Tzolzil Indian girl from the State of Chiapas is descended from generations of men and women who have struggled to survive in a harsh habitat.

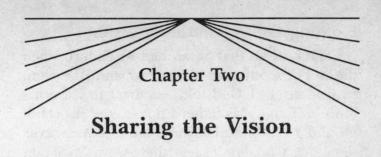

Chapter Two

Sharing the Vision

When Moses heard God in the burning bush; and, when I heard Him in the barbershop, we joined a long line of men and women who have, in solitary moments and places, received a vision of ministry. And, every person who has responded to such a vision has had to deal with sharing that vision with others, particularly family and friends. This calls for patience in both the visionary and the loved one. A process must occur during which others come to "own" the vision given by God. Such an ownership does not come easily. After all, they have not heard God speak from a burning bush; they have not been overwhelmed with His presence and given the same vision as the called person. They do not have that moment in time to look back on and say, "That was when God spoke." Our friends and loved ones have only our words to trust in, and oftentimes their faith rests in the hope that, indeed, God has spoken to us. In other words, they trust not only in God but also in us. They trust that we have heard Him. We should also realize that, oftentimes, it is harder on them than it is on us. We have received that vision. God has spoken to us.

Holding On to Another's Vision

Think of all that Sarah had to endure when the call of God came to her husband Abraham. In Genesis 12:1 God told Abraham to leave behind his family, his father's house, and his country and go in blind faith to a land he had never seen. But, God didn't speak these words to Sarah. Even though she would play a significant role in the fulfillment of God's purpose, she was not privileged to participate in this encounter between Abraham and God. Only after many years would she hear God for herself. For now, she must trust her husband.

In the same chapter, we read of Abraham bundling up all he had, gathering his immediate household and heading for Canaan. Abraham had the vision; Sarah had the submissive spirit. Just imagine what went through her mind! Would there be safety in their new home? Would she have friends? Would there be food and work available? Could they cut a new life out of this unknown land they were journeying to? Sarah was abandoning every shred of security she had in order to fulfill God's purpose in her family's life.

Some of the most difficult times for Sarah must have been when her husband began to experience questions and fear. She must have longed for the safety of her hometown when Abraham, so overcome with fear, insisted on lying about her identity, claiming she was his sister instead of his wife lest the Egyptians kill him and take her. But, even in those questioning moments, God was faithful and in His mercy protected Sarah.

In many ways Sarah reminds me of my mother. Neither of them had an easy life, yet neither of them complained. They both sacrificed for the sake of their families. I can remember my mother spending the afternoon washing clothes on a rub board, hanging them out to dry, and then cooking supper for her family. When the meal was ready, she always gave the best of the food to her husband and children and took what was left for herself. Others had white meat from chicken—or thighs or legs. Mom had the neck or the foot. Her love for her family was sacrificial. I believe Sarah was the same.

Sarah would have plenty of opportunity for discouragement in the coming years. God's word to Abraham had been that he would be the father of a great nation. But, where were the children? Where was her fertility? On one occasion she took matters into her own hands, and the result was a son for Abraham through the womb of a servant woman. Though greatly mistaken in her plotting, her desire was nevertheless praiseworthy: to see God's promise fulfilled in her husband's life.

Then one day it happened. The Angel of the Lord spoke to Abraham that Sarah would bear a son. And, Sarah heard it. Hiding behind a tent curtain, she laughed at the thought of her now old and worn body producing a baby boy. In spite of the laughing—and whether that laughing was in disbelief or sheer joy—the vision was no longer Abraham's alone. She now owned it as well. And, of course, Isaac, the little "Son of Laughter," was born to them in their old age.

The point is simply this: Sarah trusted Abraham for a great many years until the vision became hers as well. I cannot say enough about the virtue of patience. In my own life, my wife's patience paralleled that of Sarah's. Even though she did not always understand my calling, she was faithful and stood beside me through difficult times as well as glorious. Later, in a wonderful way, the vision became Mary's as well, but the time between would be filled with heartache and questions. How important it is for us to be men and women of patience as we wait and pray for those whom God has called.

A Vision Not Fully Seen

Not only does God rarely give a specific vision to more than one person at a time, He also seldom gives a complete vision in a single encounter. Abraham and Moses didn't see "the whole picture" from their first dialogues with God. God lets us see only as much as we have faith to believe. If God had shown me all that He was going to do in my ministry, I doubt that I would have accepted the call. I think that I would have said, "I can't do it, Lord. It's too big a task; get someone else." If He had shown me the Bible schools, the medical clinics and the churches that I would build—if He had shown me the financial expenditure necessary to make these things a reality—I believe my heart would have failed me for fear. If He had shown me a vision of myself floating down a river on the border of Guatemala with rifle-fire whizzing over my head, or pastors' houses being burned to the ground because of the gospel they preached, or treacherous mountain roads traveled on rainy nights, or bandits intent on robbing me of my money and, perhaps, my life—no, I don't think I could have responded with faith.

Would Moses have accepted the call if he could have seen the future—if he could have heard the people complaining and could have seen their lack of faith as they approached Canaan, or watched ahead of time as they wandered for forty years in a desert wasteland—would he have said "Yes" to God? What if Moses had seen his own brother and sister turning against him, or God's people bowing to a golden calf? But, he didn't see this. He saw only that God had called him to lead the people to freedom.

In Acts, chapter 9, we read of God calling the greatest missionary of the New Testament Church, the apostle Paul. His response to the vision was wholehearted, to the point of losing all he had achieved before this grand encounter. Little did he know what lay ahead! Years later he would reflect on his life of ministry:

> I have worked much harder, been in prison more frequently, been flogged more severely, and been exposed to death again and again. Five times I received from the Jews the forty lashes minus one. Three times I was beaten with rods, once I was stoned, three times I was shipwrecked, I spent a night and a day in the open sea, I have been in danger from rivers, in danger from bandits, in danger from my own countrymen, in danger from Gen-

tiles; in danger in the city, in danger in the
country, in danger at sea; and in danger from
false brothers. I have labored and toiled and
have often gone without sleep; I have known
hunger and thirst and have often gone without food; I have been cold and naked. Besides everything else, I face daily the pressure of my concern for all the churches (2
Cor. 11:23-28).

Having endured all this, Paul did not consider
it too great a price to pay for the sake of the
gospel of Jesus Christ. Indeed, he was willing to
pay an even greater price—that of his very life. To
his dear son in the faith he wrote,

This is a trustworthy saying that deserves full
acceptance (and for this we labor and strive),
that we have put our hope in the living God,
who is the Savior of all men, and especially
of those who believe. (1 Tim. 4:9-10) [And],
For I am already being poured out like a
drink offering, and the time has come for my
departure. I have fought the good fight, I
have finished the race, I have kept the faith.
Now there is in store for me the crown of
righteousness, which the Lord, the righteous
Judge, will award me on that day—and not
only to me, but also to all who have longed
for his appearing. (2 Tim. 4:6-8)

But he did not begin his ministry with all this
in sight. He began by saying "Yes" to the vision
God had given him.

God's Methodology in Vision

Biographies, like history, are written retrospectively. It is a recounting of what has already happened. The story is there from beginning to end before a single page has run off the press. But, God does not work like a publishing house. He does not mail us a manuscript detailing everything that is going to take place in our lives. He simply promises to be with us through the days and years of our lives and to protect us from anything we cannot bear. He promises to strengthen us in our weakness and to equip us to fulfill the vision He burns within our hearts. It is not necessary for us to see the entire picture in a single flash. We wouldn't understand it if we did. What is essential is that we trust the One who has called us to accomplish His purpose.

When I first desired to learn to build, I remember watching a new house under construction and wondering just how a carpenter could "see" the finished product in his mind: the roof line, the angles—how did he know? In my first excursions into construction I can remember worrying and fretting because I was afraid that I would not be able to get the roof right. I felt sure that I could build the walls. That would be simple: just nail the studs to the plates and raise the wall. But the roof? Well, that would be different. I just couldn't get the complete picture in my mind as to exactly how it would look.

Quite honestly, after building scores of church buildings and homes, I still haven't figured it out!

At least in my experience, it just "works." I do what needs to be done first—the raising of the walls—and the rest comes together when it is supposed to come together. If I waited until I understood every angle, I'd still be standing in front of the foundation of my very first building, never having accomplished a single thing.

I believe it works the same way when we are "building" a ministry for God. We don't see the end results exactly as they will be. We simply do what we know to do, and God brings it to completion. How marvelous it is to watch as God brings to completion those things we couldn't see when we first began. It has been such a joy to see Him bring light where there had been darkness, to watch as He provided joy for the sorrowful and life for the dying. All the work, all the sacrifices and all the not knowing pay off when God brings His plan together. I remember when Julio Maya, a young businessman from the interior of Mexico, approached the platform after a crusade in Atoyac. Putting his arms around me, he said through tears of joy, "Thank you for bringing God to us." That statement was payment in full! As I drive away from some small village in a remote area and look through the rear-view mirror at a new church building, knowing that the people have a place to worship—payment in full! When I see young people receive Christ and know they can live a blessed life—what more reward could I ask for?

An Infectious Vision

In saying yes to the call of God to go to the mission field, I also had to communicate with the church I served that I would no longer be their pastor, with my family that I would no longer have a "normal" lifestyle, and with my friends that I was taking a risk "against all odds" in becoming a missionary. In retrospect, it was the best decision I could have made. Not only would this vision affect thousands of lives in Mexico, but its infectious nature would cause it to spread to many people in the United States. Pastors would be challenged afresh as they visited the works; youth groups would leave with a deep awareness of God's love for lost people; and so many individuals, longing for fullness in their own empty souls, would find it as they served others less fortunate than themselves.

One young man who stands out in my mind was Roger, a member of a youth group visiting from Florida. With sixteen young people ranging in age from ten to eighteen, Roger found himself so touched by what he had seen in Mexico that he vowed then and there to pursue the life of a missionary. Eight years later, while visiting in Florida, I was approached at the end of a church service by a young man: "Do you remember me?" he asked. And, when I couldn't place him, he told me of the impact that trip had had on him: "I am now twenty-two, have completed college, and will be leaving soon for Japan where I will serve as a missionary." Having a vision becomes contagious. How many more Rogers have passed under my doorposts? Only eternity will tell.

The mission field seems to be a great equalizer, and we have been joined by every conceivable kind of Christian: Baptists, Roman Catholics, Assemblies of God, Methodists, Charismatics, Independents—wealthy, middle class, poor, male, female, African-American, Hispanic and white. What a joy to see God do His work, not only through but also *in* the lives of each of these individuals and groups.

I am reminded of one "mixed" group of different denominations that came to visit us. A congregation had raised the finances to build a church in Mexico, but when the work crew arrived, the pastor had not been able to join them. They were joined by several friends from another congregation, as well as that congregation's minister. We were planning to build the structure and have the absent pastor dedicate it at a later date.

As we traveled through the parched and dry desert, heading toward the small village where we would construct the church, several men began prophesying and commanding blessings. They commanded the rains to fall and to quench the thirst of this dry land. They prophesied to the rocky earth to bring forth an abundance of corn and beans. As we passed poor villages, they spoke out a curse upon the poverty, declaring in faith that by faith these people were not poor for their Father had an abundant supply.

Now, I too believe that God cares for His children, and that He is not only capable but willing to bless them. But, I also knew that this was desert we were driving through. The land was hard, and the inhabitants were descendents of generations of men and women who had fought

the desert to scrape out a survival. I didn't expect
things to change overnight. I understood that
God's purposes often work transgenerationally:
that one generation works hard and another generation builds after them. The hope I had for
these people was not that the desert would mi-
raculously blossom the next morning but that the
power of the Gospel would transform their lives,
cause them to walk in obedience to God's will,
and bring them eventual prosperity guaranteed
in his Word.

I was chided for my lack of faith by these
brothers, but our relationship remained intact,
and I was beginning to enjoy some of the person-
alities present—it was just a little embarrassing to
hear them open the doors and prophesy blessings every time we made a stop. As the work on
the church neared completion, we realized that
we were short of a few sheets of roofing tin. We
could either pitch in together and buy what was
needed, or the church would have to wait until
the next trip to have a completed roof. We were
short about two hundred dollars, and I felt sure
these men of faith could come up with the necessary funds. I presented the need and suggested
we all do our fair share to complete this task.
One by one they began to tell me of the hard
times that had fallen upon them. Besides the
pastor, there was only one other man of this group
who had a job. All of the others were unem-
ployed.

It's humorous now, but the lesson was learned:
if it doesn't work in the United States, chances

are it won't work on the mission field either.
There is one God, one faith and one gospel given
to the whole world. The reverse is also true: if the
"gospel" we are preaching in the United States
doesn't work on the mission field, we had better
stop, reflect and consider whether what we are
proclaiming is the true universal message of God's
good news.

Some months later the pastor who had raised
the money for this project had the opportunity to
dedicate the beautiful, little, block church. What
a celebration! The townspeople prepared food,
and singers and musicians led in joyous thanksgiving. When we arrived in the late afternoon,
the people graciously received us, and the American pastor rejoiced to see the good work produced by his congregation's contributions. There
was plenty of greeting and embracing; and cam-
eras were flashing as the guests took photographs
of the building and people, to share with the
faithful back home. When the service moved into
full swing, the little church was packed. Not another person could have been squeezed in; every
seat was full and people were crowded into the
aisles. At every window, faces were peering in
from the outside; and the doors were blocked
with spiritually hungry Mexicans.

Sometime during the celebrating, the American pastor had slipped away from the platform,
perhaps to go outside and get fresh air. When I
called for him to bring the sermon, he did not
respond. Again, I called; and, still, there was no
response. Concerned now that he may have been

ill from the traveling and the change in food, I made my way toward the back to find him.

I located him standing in the corner of the building, face buried in his hands and weeping intensely. When I invited him to the platform, he said he could not go. He wouldn't be able to preach, he said. I reminded him that the people were expecting his sermon and that they would be disappointed if he did not preach; nevertheless, he refused. Then, in trembling voice he said, "I came to Mexico thinking I was going to teach these people about Christ, but these people know more than I do." He came to a realization that, although poor by worldly standards, these people of faith were rich in the treasures of God. A national pastor brought the sermon while my friend continued to ponder the wonderful things he had seen.

Yes, the mission field is a great equalizer. Rich and poor, brown and white—we all become equals on the frontlines of God's Kingdom. There, on the edge of civilization, I have seen spoiled teenagers transformed into caring young people; I have seen Christians who assumed they "had it all together" humble themselves in the presence of uneducated farmers, realizing these people had a life of faith unparalleled in the comfortable churches "back home." I have seen pastors discouraged by the apathy of sullen congregations renewed with a vision for changing the world.

My desire is to encourage men and women to holy boldness as they respond to God's call in their lives. Feelings of inadequacy may arise, but

God has been preparing us all our lives to accomplish the task he sets before us. We may not have confidence in ourselves, but God has confidence in us, and we can have great confidence in Him!

I suppose young David never knew how much his slingshot training would pay off. Little did he realize that his shepherding was only preparation for being the shepherd of God's people, but God knew. God was with him when he fought the lion, when he fought the bear. God was there when he threw his first stone from his first sling. God was molding him in his life to fulfill his life's purpose. And, so He is with each of us. We are to be bold; be strong; for the Lord our God is with us!

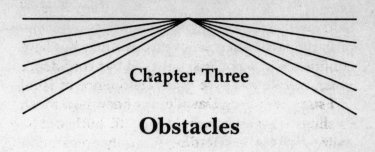

Chapter Three

Obstacles

Having made the decision to respond to the vision God had given me, to leave behind my former life and become a missionary, I now faced the difficult task of overcoming the obstacles that blocked my way. In my future lay spiritual mountains and valleys to navigate through, but there were obstacles that had to be crossed before scaling the terrain of my future was even a possibility.

No matter how I longed to fulfill God's call in my life, there were the very real and very near problems of learning a new language, raising finances, dealing with family and entering the mission field as an "old man" by most missionary-organization standards. I am convinced that many people never get past these obstacles to go on and successfully fulfill their vision.

There are two basic ways we can approach the obstacles between us and the accomplishment of our vision. We can stand still, stare at the difficulties and be overcome with fear; or we can approach these problems as a kind of obstacle course that we run through and climb over—a course that will prove to be valuable training for the work that lies ahead of us. However we approach them, the obstacles are genuine. They are not simply figments of the imagination that will go away with just a little extra wishful thinking.

The Obstacles Are Real

A few years ago, a teaching was becoming popular which declared that there was never anything really wrong in the Christian's life, that person simply had symptoms of something being wrong. A high fever that remained after prayer was not really a high fever; it was just a symptom. It was thought to be a lack of faith to say "I am sick." Instead, we were supposed to say "I have the symptoms of being sick." This kind of thinking is really nothing more than the newest manifestation of Gnosticism, an ancient error combatted in 1 John. It has been around since the first century and finds one of its modern expressions in the Christian Science movement founded by Mary Baker Eddy. I believe a pastor friend has a good response to this silly teaching. He had a beautiful young daughter studying in Bible college who dated a handsome young man also attending the school. The young lady invited her suitor to attend her home church one weekend.

On Saturday evening while she prepared for the coming day, her boyfriend and father were able to visit together and discuss, among other things, matters of the faith. The issue of symptoms vs. real problems came up, and the young man insisted that problems were only symptoms unless they were submitted to. The pastor tried to reason with him, but with no success. After a couple of hours the young man excused himself to the restroom, asking directions. The pastor ignored him and kept talking. A few minutes later the young man asked again; and once again, he was ignored. The discomfort became so intense that the young man, realizing an imminent problem, stood up and with pain in his voice said, "Please, sir: where is your restroom?" The wise pastor replied, "Sit down, son. You don't need a restroom. It's only symptoms that you are feeling!"

My friend's humor causes me to laugh to this day, but how well it shows that obstacles can't just be ignored in hopes that they will soon vanish. Difficulties that arise as we prepare for our ministry must be faced head-on, and solutions must be discovered that will eliminate the problems. In dealing with the many obstacles before me as I prepared for transition from pastoral ministry to missionary service, the one thing I needed the most was the one thing I had the least of: understanding. I didn't completely understand what was happening myself, and others certainly didn't understand. There was no moral support—not one word of encouragement; no one shared the vision or sensed what I felt burning in my spirit.

My mother and father could not understand why I would leave the church that I had worked so hard to build. My wife's parents had just as difficult a time accepting my decision. Our closest friends in the congregation said it would never work. I kept hearing questions like, "What can a

single man accomplish on the mission field?" "You
don't even have financial backing; how do you
think you are going to get to Mexico?" "Aren't
you too old to begin learning a new language?"
However, each time I heard these questions I
thought of Moses, who at the age of eighty led
Israel out of Egypt; and Caleb, who at eighty
could still say, "I'll take that mountain for my
own." Here I was, only half their age! I could do
it if God worked with me.

Getting Our House in Order

The first area that demanded my attention
was my family. Mary and I had three children:
two sons and a young adopted daughter. Ken,
my oldest son, was newly married and in Bible
college studying for the ministry. Faced with the
normal pressures of school and work, he depended on us for financial help in his education.
Paul, my youngest son, was still in high school,
looking forward to a life and career of his own.

Now our whole world was about to change.
My wife and I discussed the consequences of the
decision that we had just made. Our lives were
going to change. There would be great sacrifices
for both of us. We would no longer have a "normal" family home. We would be separated from
one another for longer periods of time than ever
before. For the first time in our married life, my
wife and I would be separated while I "went to
work"—at first, only days at a time, then weeks
and months. The demands on Mary were as strong
as the demands on me: she would be responsible
for the raising of our family when I was away,

and she would have limited financial resources to supply the family's needs.

I should say here that I did not enter the missionary work under ideal circumstances, and I do not encourage anyone else to do it just like I did. There are better ways. It would have been better to have had the backing of a denomination or church. It would have been better to have trained in the language. It would have been better to have been twenty years younger—but these were not options available to me. If there is a better way—a way without as many difficulties—by all means, take it. Nevertheless, when God calls, we take the best path available at the time.

A Partner in the Face of Obstacles

All the obstacles surrounding a change of life didn't disappear after a month or two. There were adjustments to be made that took years to complete. Until I went to the mission field, I was the family member responsible for handling our personal finances. Now I wouldn't be home, and this responsibility would fall to Mary.

I can't say enough about my wife, and what a partner she has been through the thick and thin of missionary life. Little did she know on the spring day in 1957 just what her words "for better or worse, for richer for poorer" would mean! Even though in the beginning she was not inspired with the vision for foreign missions like I was, she remained a faithful, supportive helper in all that I did. Never once did she complain or question the validity of my vision—even though I am sure she must have wondered inwardly about the wisdom of my decisions. How she fulfilled her own calling to be a supportive wife! I could not have asked for a more wonderful spouse, and God could not have given me a better one. I heard a radio preacher say that if Adam hadn't liked Eve, God would have made him another mate! That's not theologically sound, but I give thanks that my first choice was the perfect choice.

Soon after I opted for the mission field, our second son, Paul, married, leaving Mary and Gina at home alone. Gina was now approaching teen years; her life was becoming complicated. We never completely severed ties with her biological mother and grandparents; and now, they were coming back into the scene, stirring up confusion and dividing loyalties. Gina desired to visit them more and more frequently, and then asked to live with them. After consultation with lawyers, and much prayer, we decided it would be best for her to return to her biological family. Now, with Ken away, Paul married and Gina returning to her family, our home was left with only Mary and me—and much of the time I was away.

Enough transition for one family to endure, we thought. Little did we know that even greater changes lay ahead. While pastoring in Denison, we had purchased fifty acres in the country where we built a new home overlooking woods and pastureland. Our property adjoined Mary's parents' property, and even with the children and myself away, Mary always had her mother for companionship. But, only a few short years later, Thelma died after suffering from cancer. The blow was devastating to Mary; now she felt completely alone. The nights were the most difficult for Mary, when memories flooded her mind. Her only solace was to busy herself during the day and spend evenings with friends, visiting as long as possible and returning home only to sleep.

While Mary suffered through her pain, sometimes in my presence, sometimes in my absence, I too was going through the most difficult era of my life. Finances were poor, support was thin, the demands were great; and sometimes, I didn't think I could take it all. There were moments of depression when I wished for death. For the first time in my life I did not belong to anything. I had no "real" job. I had always earned my way before—as a barber, I had a regular clientele and dear friends; as a pastor, I had loving parishioners and close associates. I felt as if I had value and worth in those days. Now, no one was praising me. No one was supportive of my work. Even my family seemed to not need me anymore: both boys now had their own lives, and Mary was beginning to adjust very well to the nonpastoral role of involvement in an area church. What turmoil for me! I didn't feel comfortable visiting the church I had pastored, yet I found it very difficult to belong to any other congregation—even the one Mary was becoming committed to. Although the church would later become a strong supporter of our ministry, in the early years I felt very much alone, without friend or peer.

As if it wasn't enough to be going through both spiritual and emotional midlife crises, at the same time I was finding myself sleeping on dirt floors in adobe huts in the middle of Mexico. And now that I was here, what was I to do? I usually had just enough money to get me where I was going and back home—and very little with which to do actual work. When money had depleted, I would return home, scrape and save for my next trip. During this "hand-to-mouth" period of time, my excursions into Mexico were short—usually only a few days—because I couldn't afford to stay a single day longer.

In spite of all these difficulties, I never lost sight of the vision. I knew I had been born to be a missionary. It was my call, my destiny. I had been prepared for this all my life; and with God's help, I was determined that it would become a reality. I knew that if I persevered, someone would eventually believe in me, share my vision. I also knew that God believed in me even during the darkest days. The love in my heart for the people of Mexico began to increase, and opportunities to share it increased as well.

On one occasion I visited a desert village with Jerry McSorley, a missionary friend who had built several churches in the area and who helped get me started in missionary work. The church was small, and the pastor lived with his family of seven in a two-room house adjoining the church. The "kitchen" was outside, and the stove was a fifty-five-gallon barrel that was filled with wood. The roofline of the house looked like an exaggerated "sway-backed" horse that had been ridden too much; and every time it rained, the family endured leaks through the entire home. When evening came, Jerry and I slept on the church floor. The following morning we arose to the sound of the pastor's wife preparing tortillas and two eggs over the barrel stove. Her husband returned from the village with a small can of sardines intended to round off our breakfast. As this meager fare was set before us, we found it difficult to eat—not because of the poverty of the meal—but because five little children were standing nearby watching us. These poor people were doing their best to show hospitality, even at the cost of their own children remaining hungry. I knew that I needed to eat something to avoid offending our host, so I ate an egg and a tortilla. When I had finished with our breakfast I watched as the children lined up for their food. The mother took a single sardine, pressed it into a tortilla, and gave one to each child. How my heart burned to help these people! Whatever cost must be paid, it would be worth it. Later I returned with seven hundred dollars, built an additional room and replaced the roof on the home. With no electricity or lumber, we literally built the room and roof with machete and hammer.

A Proverbial Lone Ranger

One of the great obstacles I faced in the early years of ministry was not having the support or backing of a group. At the age of forty, I had already passed the acceptable age of appointment in the Assemblies of God; in short, I was too old to become a missionary. This meant that I could not be an "official" Assemblies of God missionary, nor could I represent my missionary work as sanctioned by the denomination. I would not be able to visit churches and raise support with the full blessing of the church. This made a tremendous difference in the ability to raise finances for various works. Officially appointed missionaries could itinerate throughout the United States, presenting their needs and raising financial commitments. These offerings would be credited by the Assemblies of God as recognized foreign mission offerings. But, since I was not appointed, contributions to my work would not be recognized and the churches making the contributions could not officially claim them as foreign mission giving.

Having been ordained with the Assemblies of God for sixteen years before beginning missionary work, and having kept this ordination as I ventured into a new field of ministry, I at first assumed that my many "connections" with fellow pastors and denominational friends would be a source of some moral and financial support. But, how little I knew of human nature and the workings of denominational politics! How quickly I was forgotten, even by my closest pastor friends with whom I had attended various district meetings. Some had hunted and fished with me, some had shared my pulpit, but now it felt like I was sitting outside their gates crying "Unclean! Unclean!" I had apparently contacted the leprous disease of "nonaffiliation."

I recognize that the Assemblies of God are no exception to the rule and that practically all denominations operate in a similar way, but I do wish that we could all broaden our way of thinking and move beyond the denominational barriers into a mindset of expanding the Kingdom of God. Jesus taught us to take the gospel to the nations. I suggest we tear down the barriers that prevent this from happening.

Perhaps the most disappointing occasion of collegial abandonment came after I had built a number of churches in Mexico and a Bible school near Acapulco. During one of my visits home, I shared some slides and the story of my ministry with the teenage Sunday school class of a local Assemblies of God church. The scheduled speaker for the morning service was a district official whom I had known for years, who also directed the foreign missions division of our district. The official sat in the Sunday school class and afterwards, over lunch, said he was very impressed with what I had been doing in Mexico. He invited me to join him in a sectional meeting a few weeks later, when several Assemblies missionaries representing many countries would be assembled. He said he would like to take the time to recognize me and give me the opportunity to explain my ministry to my peers. How exciting! Perhaps the years of isolation were ending! I eagerly accepted the invitation and then, that very afternoon, began the long drive back to the Acapulco area where I continued to work on the Bible school.

The three-day drive back home would be long and tiresome, and the only reason for the return trip would be to attend this missionary meeting; but it would be worth it if I could find camaraderie. When the meeting date finally arrived, I sat on the pew behind the district official who had so kindly invited me. After the morning sermon all the missionaries were invited to share lunch in the fellowship hall, and the tables were arranged in a U-shape to accommodate conversation. A podium was placed at the end of the tables, from which each missionary was given a few minutes to speak. I enjoyed hearing the wonderful things God was doing. One by one these men of God shared their hearts until, finally, we were asked to stand and be dismissed. My name was never called. I was never asked to speak. My work was never even recognized. I had made the grueling three-day drive for nothing.

In later years the work in Mexico was embraced by many denominations. Men and women from every background came together, working with others to further the Kingdom of God. In later years I was warmly received, not because of my denominational nametag, but because the ministry was bearing fruit. But, those early years taught me a great lesson: I have determined to never allow the churches in Mexico to become exclusive, but to always keep a "kingdom-view" perspective on life and ministry. Not wanting to develop a ministry without accountability, I surrounded myself with a board of directors—men who were committed to the vision of foreign missions, who had joined me on several occasions in Mexico, and who could help give me balance and direction as the work began to grow.

Speaking in an Unknown Tongue—Como?

As if all this weren't difficult enough, I began working in Mexico without knowing the Spanish language. In the normal pattern of things, a young missionary trains in language school, raises support and prepares in every way before heading out for a foreign field. But, I couldn't itinerate, so there were no funds; and I couldn't pack my bags and go to school, so there was no language learned. I knew I didn't have to speak Spanish in order to drive a nail, and I knew I could carry cement blocks and mix concrete without conversational skills. And, that is exactly what I did! My friend Jerry McSorley who already had twenty years of missionary experience under his belt invited me to work with him, and I couldn't refuse the open door. The first several trips into Mexico were with Jerry. He had built a number of churches throughout the country, and he welcomed me to work and help in any way I could. Certainly I could not assist in preaching or teaching or evangelism, but I could build churches. To this day, construction is still the part of the missionary work that I enjoy most.

After many trips into Mexico with Jerry McSorley, it was time for me to spread my wings and make a trip alone. A tiny church located about one hundred miles south of Saltillo needed gable ends in the roof. What would be a half-day job in the United States took three days in this little village, where I worked without electricity and with only a poor selection of lumber. With handsaw, machete, and hammer, this was going to be a major accomplishment!

Driving 550 miles from my home to my son's home in Zapata, Texas, I then switched vehicles with him and drove a small Toyota the rest of the way. I intended to stay the night at a Bible school in Saltillo and get a fresh start the next morning, but having only visited it once, I was unable to find it again. Without money for a hotel, I drove on through the night to my destination. Around one o'clock in the morning I turned off the main highway and began traveling down a rough desert road to reach the village. I decided to sleep in the car until daybreak and continue the last leg of my journey in the light. I pulled off the road and parked in front of a little building hoping to get some rest. All night long the big trucks zoomed past on the nearby highway, and the little Toyota provided minimal room to stretch. Needless to say, I didn't sleep very well.

The next morning I awoke at daybreak and discovered that the little building I had parked in front of was a restaurant. I went in to enjoy a good breakfast before facing a hard day of work. As I walked in, every eye in the place turned to search out this "gringo" who suddenly intruded on their morning. A young lady came over and asked me something in a language that I certainly couldn't understand. I sat there looking dumbfounded as the stares became more intense. Jerry had taught me to say "huevos" when ordering eggs, and that was all I knew to say. When the waitress again asked for my order (I assume that's what she was asking for), I said, "Dos huevos"— two eggs. She asked something else, and having no idea what she said I responded, "Si."

A few minutes later the woman returned with two raw eggs in a glass, accompanied by a wedge of lemon. I looked around and noticed others had ordered the same thing. They had stirred the eggs together and squeezed the lemon juice into the glass. They were drinking their breakfast. Acting like I did this every morning, I carefully stirred my eggs, squeezed in the lemon juice and started to down my morning meal. When the first drop of this concoction touched my lips, I knew it couldn't go any further! I left the drink on the table and escaped from the restaurant as quickly as I could. I can imagine the laughs those folks had after I made my way out the door!

During sixteen years of pastoral ministry, I had a lot of "preach" in me. I was always ready with a sermon; and anytime I could find an interpreter, I was prepared to bring the people a message. During one period I went without preaching longer than I was comfortable. There seemed to be no one around to interpret for me, so I finally found a young man who spoke about as much English as I did Spanish. With this precarious situation, I decided to preach God's Word to the congregation in a Tex-Mex style, a little English and a little Spanish.

I was rolling along nicely when I came upon the word "being." I was speaking of the nature of a person, his very being, and it was being interpreted as "frijoles"! Soon everyone was laughing—I was laughing, the interpreter was giggling, and the whole congregation was in uproar. But, God's Word proved true: "A merry heart does good like a medicine."

Another young missionary was comparing the joy of the Lord with the sweetness of honey in a honeycomb. Each time he would make the comparison, the congregation would crack up. It turned out the word for honeycomb is "panel," and the word for baby diaper is "pan~el." He was actually saying, "Come and taste the sweetness that flows from the baby diaper!"

The hilarity of the language barrier is part of the life of a missionary. I don't know how many truck loads of "flour" I have ordered for mixing cement, or how many times I've ordered "sand" tortillas to eat. The difference is "harina" and "arena."

Speaking Spanish poorly has its drawbacks, but so does a little fluency. There are times when ignorance is bliss, particularly when crossing the border. Most Mexican border guards speak very little English and consequently make short work of interviewing non-Spanish-speaking travelers. On my early trips I spoke to the guards in English because I knew no Spanish. Later, I began communicating with them in the little Spanish I had picked up, but this proved to be a mistake. They would then question me about everything because they were comfortable in their own language.

On one occasion I needed to carry across the border a well pump, a pressure tank, and some pvc pipe. I devised a great plan: I crammed all the materials into my van and covered it up with suitcases and blankets. With several passengers lying over the suitcases, it might just work. Then for the master stroke: "When we reach the border," I told my companions, "I will play dumb. I'll pretend I don't speak Spanish. Hopefully the guard will just wave us through." Everyone agreed this was indeed a brilliant plan. We arrived at the border, pulled through the check point and watched as a big guard made his way to us. Not to worry, we set our plan in action. The guard asked the obvious question, "What do you have in the van?" I responded, "I don't speak Spanish." Again he asked, "What do you have in the van?" Again I responded, "I don't speak Spanish." I noticed the tension building in my companions. It grew suddenly quiet and cold in the van. The guard said a third time, "What do you have in the van?" Then, it dawned on me: he was speaking perfect English! I sat there, egg on my face, too embarrassed to say anything and fearful that the van would explode in laughter at any moment. Too frustrated to deal with us, the guard waved us through and walked away.

Though frustrating, the inability to speak Spanish provided needed moments of comic relief. I had faced so many obstacles in the beginning that these times of laughter did indeed work like a medicine. How much better it would have been if I could have attended school and learned the language instead of being forced to pick it up bit by bit. I learned to point a lot in those early days, and I developed my own unique brand of sign language. I made a lot of mistakes, but they were overlooked because people knew I had good intentions. I also learned to laugh at myself a bit more freely! My main goal was to get a point

across and get a job done. Looking back, its a
wonder I finished anything in those days!

Money—Or The Lack Thereof

People say that in business, money is the
bottom line. In missions, money is the bottom
line, the top line, and every line in between. It
would take money to keep our home operating.
It would take money for travel to and from
Mexico. It would take money for work projects,
however small. It would take money for helping
pastors. It would take money for running a Bible
school and a medical clinic. Trying to stretch the
small amount of finances with which we began
would prove to be one of our greatest challenges.

Isn't it interesting how some people think of
money? When they find themselves in need,
money is very important; but when others are in
need, well, they can get by without it. I will never
forget the great "spiritual wisdom" that a visiting
businessman bestowed on one of my associates.
Tom and Deanna Shaffer had responded to God's
call for missionary service and were working with
me in Atoyac, near Acapulco. Tom and his family
had left lucrative positions in the medical world
and were scratching out a meager existence as
they served God on the mission field. A visiting
pastor had brought his businessman friend to view
the works, and one hot afternoon we all sat outside hoping for a cool breeze to blow by and
relieve the heat.

As I listened to Tom pour his heart out to the
pastor and his guest, I was amazed to hear the

businessman respond, "What you need is prayer. I would rather pray for you than give you money." I kept my mouth shut; but I wanted to say, "If you would only give Tom something you wouldn't have to pray. You could *be* an answer to his prayer instead!" The very thing they had been praying for could have been easily met that hot afternoon in Mexico. Missionary work teaches us to be very practical in our spiritual walk, never only saying kind words when a helping hand is what's needed.

Prayers are very important to the work of ministry, and I constantly ask for solid prayer support in our newsletters. Many cannot give financially but uphold us daily in prayer, and this is so desperately needed. However, we must be realistic in prayer. Part of the prayer support must be intercession for financial blessings. Money buys food. Money buys lumber. Money buys Bibles and books and medicine. When I was about fourteen I went hunting one day and returned without success. I told my father of all the tracks and signs of game I had seen. Dad looked at me and said, "Tracks make a mighty thin gravy." Prayer without giving makes a mighty thin gravy.

Every obstacle faced in responding to the vision was compounded by lack of finances. If I had had sufficient funds, our family life would have been different; people would have been more understanding of the new venture, and the fresh missionary endeavors would have been more successful. Without financial security I found myself in a vicious circle: if I held a job I could not travel to Mexico. If I traveled, I could not hold a job.

One thing I learned in pastoring was what not
to do. I didn't know exactly what to do, but I
knew some things I shouldn't do. On one occasion during my pastorate, a young member of
the church decided he was called to the ministry.
Before I could respond to him, he had sold everything and headed out to preach. He had no
preparation, no connections, no place to minister, no affiliation. To make matters worse, he had
little or no walk with God, and I wasn't even
convinced of his salvation. Later I discovered that
he had heard a preacher say, "Sell all and follow
Jesus"; so he did. Needless to say, in a few short
weeks he was back in town trying to scrape together enough furniture to start life over again. I
remembered this incident later when God began
calling me to missions. Whatever else I did, I was
committed to caring for my family. Mary and I
were both willing to make the necessary sacrifices, but there were some things that were essential for us to care for: our monthly house payments, auto payments and other bills must be
paid. Living expenses for food and clothing must
be provided. We could cut corners, but we were
committed to being responsible.

With this primary commitment to caring for
the family, there also came a commitment to set
aside funds for missionary work. If I was going to
call myself a missionary, I had to go to the mission field; and this required money. In a very real
way, people want to see fruit before they sow into
your field. I had to come up with finances for our
first few projects without the assistance of others.

This would provide a plowing of the field into which others could sow their seed.

Oftentimes this meant short trips into Mexico, spending what I had saved and returning a few days later. It also meant sleeping in cars, in churches, and on the ground. I actually even spent the night at one of the most expensive hotels in Acapulco—the Princess—on the golf course parking lot, that is. During this time my tent became my security blanket. No matter how bleak the situation, I always had a tent to crawl into and hide from the rest of the world.

The sacrifices made were actually quite insignificant compared to the joy of responding to God's call. I found that, for every problem I faced, God provided a solution. When I first traveled in Mexico, I enjoyed returning home and watching a little "brainless" television. One popular television action show, "The A-Team", sent a crew of mercenaries on missions that always seemed to have insurmountable odds. I always loved the end of the show when, after a smashing success, the captain of the team would say, "I love it when a plan comes together!"

I know the feeling. How often I've wondered how it would all work out; yet, God has come through every time. His plan always comes together.

These Tzetal Indians walked twelve miles to attend the Bible school at Chiapas.

Chapter Four

Accomplishing the Vision

I was sitting on a front porch of a house in Atoyac when I saw him hopping across the yard. Something in my heart hurt for him. He should have been soaring high in the heavens or perched in the top of a tall pine tree. But, here in Julio's front yard, hopped a beautiful young eagle—the victim of someone's wing-clipping scheme of domestication. As I lay in the hammock, I watched this marvelous creature of God make its way along the ground toward a pine tree; and with pity, I wondered what it would do once it had reached its destination. How like a man in prison was this bird—longing for the freedom it was designed to have!

When it finally reached the big tree, the eagle milled around underneath, contemplating its heights. The low-lying branches were out of reach, and it appeared to me that the eagle was destined to live out its tragic existence on the same level with chickens, scratching for worms and bugs. As I watched, the eagle hopped forward, leapt upward and, falling short of his mark, fell back to the ground. Several more attempts ended in the same failure. How I knew the longings within the eagle—to do what it was designed by God to do, yet facing obstacles that prevented it from accomplishing its purpose. My heart ached to help him up into the tree where he could view the world with an eagle's eye. I wanted to pick him up and place him on the highest limb, knowing he couldn't reach it by himself.

Suddenly, with a great burst of energy, this majestic bird made an upward thrust and landed on the lowest branch of the tree. I was beside myself! I wanted to give the bird a standing ovation right then and there. But, he wasn't finished yet—with another great leap, he reached the second limb. The eagle continued a slow process of climbing. After watching a long period of time as the eagle scaled four or five branches, I began to grow drowsy in the afternoon heat and fell asleep in the hammock. As soon as I awoke from my nap I looked around for the eagle. He wasn't in the tree, so I looked around on the ground—no eagle there, either. I stepped off the porch for a more thorough search and what caught my eye raised the hair on my neck: there sat the eagle, perched on the very top branch of the pine tree! He had made it. Whereas, I rejoiced in this creature reaching the lowest branch, with determination it had reached the highest. The eagle now sat where eagles were supposed to sit. Against all odds, he had made it. If I hadn't watched the process, I would have thought certainly that this beautiful bird had flown to the top of the tree from some distant point of origin. Since that day

God had used the eagle as a constant reminder to me that obstacles are surmountable. I had learned a lesson from the eagle: although there may be handicaps, we can be what God designed us to be.

Overcoming the Financial Obstacle

As I have already pointed out, although there were many obstacles in the early part of Mexico Ministries, the common thread that wound through them all was the lack of financial support. This single problem served as a root for so many other problems that I knew it must be dealt with first. Like the eagle committed to climbing the pine tree, I began embracing the obstacles and dealing with them one by one. The obstacle that loomed the largest—finances—was one of the first I attacked.

I began by inviting a few close friends to our home for an evening meal and explaining what I felt God wanted to do in my life. These were friends who knew me well, who after a bit of explanation would trust me, and even if they did not fully understand, would support me in friendship and prayer. That evening after dinner I poured out my heart and told these dear friends all that I sensed God calling me to. Just before leaving, someone in the group suggested an offering be taken. That night I received my first missionary offering of $250! With this first seed and a little of my own, I took off for Mexico. It would allow for a short stay, but it was a beginning. As the trips became more frequent and longer, word of our work began to spread, and others began to take interest. Our finances slowly but steadily increased as did our prayer support. We were no longer thought of as fanatics abandoning all security to chase a dream, but instead people began to see the value of what we did and began to join with us in prayer, fundraising and building projects. One friend would tell another and begin a chain reaction that continues to this day. One businessman would enlist the support of another, and small pockets of supporters began to spring up all across the United States. Each new friend meant an expansion of God's Kingdom in Mexico.

Mary Owns the Vision

For the next several months, Mary and I discussed the changes in our lives. We knew there would be times of separation, and there would be adjustments to be made. We compared our future lives to those in the secular fields who find themselves separated from family for a long period of time: offshore oil rig workers, traveling salesmen, truck drivers. If these could do it in order to make money, surely we could do it for the sake of Christ.

The first few years proved to be difficult years for Mary . One of the things that made the transition bearable for her, apart from her great love and commitment, was the reports I constantly brought back from Mexico. When I told her stories of lives touched, she would weep. She became a strong pillar of prayer as she petitioned

God for finances for various projects on the mission field, and she rejoiced with me as God answered the prayers. She never asked me to stay when she knew I had to leave. She always supported me, not only with words but with actions—packing for my trips, seeing me off, and being there with a warm home when I returned.

After five years of faithfulness to my vision through very difficult experiences, Mary began to "own" the vision herself. She began to have a desire, not only for my success, but for the mission work itself. Her occasional visits to Mexico began to take on a deeper sense of purpose. The work was no longer mine alone; we began to share the vision. One trip to Mexico serves as a turning point in my life.

We were in Atoyac, a city about an hour away from Acapulco, where I had built a Bible school and church. Mary had visited this area before and was here when we held our first crusade in the city. She had carried money here for the purchase of land, so she was not unfamiliar with the work or the people in this place. But, something different happened on this trip. At the end of the evening service, people gathered in the front to pray and seek a more intimate walk with Christ. After praying with a number of people, I noticed that only a few remained at the front of the church. Overwhelmed by the working of the Holy Spirit, I sat down on the platform step and began to weep. After a few minutes, I felt a hand on my shoulder and looked up as Mary sat beside me. We wept together and she said, "I know now what you have been feeling in your heart." From that moment on we would be one in calling and ministry.

My wife proved to be a vital asset to our missionary work. She occasionally traveled with me in Mexico, but her real ministry was back in the office in our home in Denison. From there she mailed the monthly newsletters, corresponded with friends of the ministry and arranged speaking engagements in various churches. Each trip made to Florida or Tennessee or Texas served not only to help raise financial support, but also as wonderful occasions for Mary and me to be together. It seems that God blessed us in some special way on each tour we made.

Prior to one trip to Florida, Mary had made reservations for a motel we considered within our budget. Arriving in Orlando in the afternoon, we crossed the city to our motel, and I remained in the car while Mary went in to register. She immediately returned, saying one of the pastors had called our motel leaving word that reservations had already been made for us at the Peabody Hotel. Now, I had never heard of the Peabody. I was tired from driving and wasn't very excited about another trip across town. I told Mary that the Peabody sounded like some off-brand motel and that there was no telling what condition we would find it in, but that we should go anyway since the pastor had gone to the trouble of making reservations (and this wasn't a vacation). As we neared the address of our unknown hotel, we began watching for a sign. Then we saw it: a huge, luxurious hotel that was one of the most beautiful I had ever seen—a five-star-rated palace, frequented by the world's elite when they visit Orlando! The manager was a member of the local church where I would be speaking, and he had arranged for us to stay the entire time free of charge. Mary and I felt like Ruth as she gleaned grain from the fields of Boaz and found "handfuls on purpose" that had been left for her. Blessings like these made our trips together very special times of recourse from the harsh life on the mission field.

Others Join the Parade

I wish I could tell you that everyone else caught the vision just like Mary did. For many friends it would take much longer; and for some, the vision would never be their own. Mary's mother was the only one of our parents who worked hard to understand our choices. She was a spiritual woman and could see things from a spiritual perspective while others saw only in the natural. About the time Mary "caught" the vision, her mother passed away. The one family member who halfway understood us was gone. My parents looked at the natural side of things and worried for our sake, but they too died within two years of Mary's mother's death.

Mary's father, a no-nonsense practical man who lived through the hard times of the depression and World War II, is the only parent left with us. At the time of this writing he is eighty years old and, after all these years, still sees no sense at all

in my working in Mexico. "There are plenty of
lost people right here in the United States!" he
tells me. When I speak of being called to the
Mexican people he tells me that there are plenty
of them living in the United States also, and there's
just no need for me to go all the way down to
Mexico. My father-in-law is joined in his lack of
understanding by some acquaintances who—after
seeing the fruit of hundreds of new churches,
several Bible schools and medical clinics and over
two hundred pastors—still do not recognize the
validity of our work. Time, however, has a way of
proving a thing, and in time more of our friends
have begun to embrace our ministry.

With each new trip into Mexico I picked up
new Spanish words, new cultural understanding,
and new ways to relate to the people. Each new
trip produced good reports of God's handiwork
among the people of Mexico, and every good
report seemed to generate new interest in individuals and congregations. Invitations to speak
began to increase, and God added partners to
our work.

The Good Reward of Hard Work

I believe the single most important element in
our financial turn-around was the time-honored
and biblically sound principle of success by hard
work. I agree with the advertisement for the Smith-
Barney investment group: "We make money the
old-fashioned way: we earn it." Too many people
assume that serving God involves simply sitting
in an easy chair waiting for Him to make all the

provisions. I have found that God provides when we get into the harvest and start doing the work we are called to do.

Many years ago I heard a preacher illustrate his sermon on the work ethic with the story of the farmer standing in his beautiful field. A stranger happened by and said to the farmer, "My, what a beautiful field you have. Hasn't God done wonders with it!" To which the farmer replied, "You should have seen it when God had it by himself." God called Adam to subdue the earth. He called the apostles to disciple the nations. Both callings still stand for Christians, and both are accomplished only with sweat and hard work.

I was willing to do everything within my ability to raise finances for Mexico Ministries. I never turned down an invitation to speak in any church. It mattered not what the denomination was nor how small the congregation was; if they were interested in missions and would let me tell my story, I was more than happy to accommodate them. Oftentimes, I would drive several hours to speak to a small group of believers, not knowing whether even my traveling expenses would be covered. Sometimes I walked away with a deficit, but sometimes God would bless far beyond my expectations. Always I enlisted godly people to lift our ministry in prayer.

We also established a mailing list to send out a monthly newsletter to our friends, and I was determined from the beginning to make these letters personal and positive. On one occasion, I was approached by a minister offering to sell me ten thousand addresses and a mailing system. He told me that it was a proven fact that a certain percentage of recipients would respond. I refused his offer on the spot. I wanted our letters to be personal, to be positive, and to be meaningful to those who received them. To this day we send out a limited number of letters, only to those who have shown an interest in the ministry in Mexico.

The Mistake of Divided Loyalties

Even with the newsletter and the few speaking engagements, we would still fall short of the money we needed to be full-time missionaries. I thought of several ways to help out the cause. I built a small grocery store, thinking that the income from the store would enable me to spend more time in Mexico. This proved to be a mistake from the beginning. The store took all of my time, and I had none left for the mission field. I wasn't skilled in this kind of business and wasn't prepared for the shock of finances lost due to shoplifting. I found myself getting nowhere fast and sold the business in less than a year. I licked my wounds and continued forward.

My brother-in-law was proprietor of a well-established barbershop that I had originally started many years ago. He understood my predicament and agreed to give me a space to cut hair while I waited for increased opportunities of ministry. This proved to be a very difficult time for me, feeling like the eagle with clipped wings (snipping hair while dreaming of Mexico). Matters were complicated when long-time acquaintances would

come in for a haircut and ask, "Did you quit the
ministry and go back into barbering?" Many times
I had to explain my plan when customers would
say, "I thought you resigned the church to go to
the mission field! Why are you here cutting hair?"
In spite of the questions, barbering supplied finances for my family and allowed me to save
enough to take those occasional trips into Mexico.
As friends began to assist in the work of ministry,
the haircuts became fewer, and the trips became
more frequent.

God continued to provide both through the
sweat of my brow and His own unexpected miraculous intervention. There were times when I
would think a task impossible or the finances
unavailable; and from out of nowhere, God would
provide. It was as if He were saying, "We're in
this together. I am with you." God's blessing our
ministry gave me great faith to believe for the
many needs we would face as we walked the
missionary road.

When it's all said and done, it is God who
receives all glory for the accomplishments of
ministry. Yes, one man can make a difference,
but that must be one man working under the
grace, empowerment and inspiration of the Holy
Spirit. It is actually God who makes all the difference. And so, in spite of my hard work and long
hours, the real supply for our ministry needs
would come from somewhere else—a place where
the vision blossomed into a wonderful reality.

Chapter Five

Building the Team

When Solomon requested one thing of God—it was wisdom, which evidenced that he had the beginning of it before he even asked. My prayer has always been that God would give me favor with men. The Bible tells us that, through his teen-age and early adult years, Jesus "grew in stature and in favor with all men." I have taken this verse as a regular prayer: "O God, give me favor with people. Give me favor with the Mexican people. Give me favor with American supporters. Give me favor with pastors on both sides of the border. Give me favor with men and women who will share the vision you have given me."

From the beginning I have known that if I found favor with people, I could accomplish what God wanted done in my life. An essential part of fulfilling the vision burning in my heart was surrounding myself with men and women who would stand with me on both sides of the Rio Grande, making a team that would bridge that river with the good news of Jesus' love.

Favor with a Businessman

When God answers my prayers for favor with men, I usually have nothing to do with it. It seems that He, in His sovereignty, brings certain people into my life that are exactly the people needed to build the ministry team. One of these persons is Paul Pogue, a successful businessman in Sherman, Texas. Although many businessmen and women have joined the ranks of our supporters, Paul is unique. He is not only a significant financial contributor; he is also a dear friend, and one who shares a burden for worldwide missions.

When we first began our relationship, Paul was a young commercial building contractor in Sherman, ten miles south of my hometown of Denison, Texas. He knew nothing of my work in Mexico, and I had never heard of him. He and his wife Judy had taken a vacation to the resort city of Zihuatanejo, about four hours north of Acapulco. After a few days of rest and relaxation, they decided to rent a car and drive to Acapulco. Halfway between these two cities, the couple came through the small town of Coyuca. As he stopped near a river to photograph the women washing their laundry on the rocks, Paul heard God speak to him. Judy confirmed that God was calling them to help the people of Mexico. Ironically (but not coincidentally!) at that very moment I was less than thirty miles from them, just beginning to build the Bible school in Atoyac. These soon-to-be-friends actually passed within five miles of where I was working!

When the Pogues returned from their vacation, Judy and Mary (who had been attending the same church) had lunch together, and Mary told her all about our fledgling missionary work. An invitation was extended for them to join us for dinner upon my return from Mexico, and within a few weeks Paul and Judy were sitting at our dining room table discussing the work of God. That evening our hearts were bonded together in love for the people of Mexico. That was ten years ago, and since then, the bond has only increased.

From the very beginning, Paul recognized that his calling in life was not to pack his bags and go on the mission field, but to remain in the construction business and create a supply line to missionaries in various parts of the world. As he honored this calling, God began to bless his work, and our two fields of ministry—construction business and missions—seemed to grow together from small works to significant institutions.

But, personal financial involvement was not enough for Paul. He had a vision to involve other businessmen in the ministry. Trip after trip, Paul would bring guests to Mexico and show them the handiwork of God. Many were moved as they witnessed firsthand the incredible moving of God among the poverty-stricken people, and many became faithful supporters of our work. As the years passed our ministry doubled, then doubled again, and the same happened with Paul's business. It seemed as though God had a plan (I love it when a plan comes together!).

Having a friend like Paul does not mean that there are never testing times financially. We are still called to step out in faith and trust God to meet our needs. Many times I have made promises to the people of Mexico, not knowing exactly how I would fulfill those promises, but in every situation God has always provided. In the fifteen years I have been in missionary work, I have been able to keep every commitment I have made. The needs have not always been met exactly as I expected them to be, but God has always come through in wonderful ways. I've often said that when I see God, I'm going to ask Him why He made me "sweat it out" so many times, living down to the last minute without knowing how He would solve a problem. But, He has never failed me yet, and I have confidence that His provisions will continue in the future.

Our Louisiana Cohorts

On one tour of churches in the United States, we were nearing the end and still facing a great need for three thousand dollars to build a small mission. Usually, I think I have a pretty good idea of where needs will be met, and usually I am wrong! I was confident that the need would be met because the last service of the tour was at a large church in south Louisiana that has faithfully supported our ministry. Arriving in the area a few days early to visit with friends, we called the church office to inform them of our arrival. Then came the shocking news: the church had accidentally double-scheduled the service, and we had been canceled. The promised three thousand dollars mission was now in jeopardy. With no more services scheduled, I didn't know how God was going to meet our need this time.

Rather than crying over spilled milk, we continued our journey, stopping to enjoy a visit with our friends Lee and Nell Lamury—he, pastor of a wonderful church in Morgan City—and both, faithful supporters of Mexico Ministries. Lee, who had planned a gourmet Cajun feast of boiled crawfish for the evening, informed me that we would be joined by another couple he had invited, and that this was an opportunity to make new friends.

A few minutes before dinner, the doorbell rang and Lee introduced me to Alex Armond and Carolyn Cutrone. We visited around the meal and talked of Mexico as we applied the Cajun-bred skill of shucking "crawdads." We continued our fellowship until late in the evening when Alex and Carolyn bid farewell. But, not ten minutes had gone by when the doorbell rang again, and to our surprise, there stood Alex and Carolyn! Had there been car trouble? Did they forget something?

As we all sat down together again Alex informed us that, although they had left earlier, God was not finished with our meeting yet. He then reached over and handed me a one-hundred-dollar bill. As he did, I noticed Carolyn writing a check which she handed to Pastor Lee, telling him to build a church in Mexico with the fund. I could hardly contain myself when Lee handed me the check written out for seven thousand dollars! Once again, God had provided for us above and beyond our need, and just in the nick of time.

Alex and Carolyn later married and became very close friends to Mary and me. They have continued to stand with us in friendship, prayer, and financial support. And, we still enjoy good Cajun food with the Armonds and the Lamurys. Visiting these dear friends in Morgan City is a kind of returning home for me—for the very river that flows through the city is the river I grew up on. Where once the river provided for our needs through wild game and fishing, it now provided us with great partners in the work of God.

Healers in Our Midst

As the ministry in Mexico continued to grow, it became clear that financial and prayer support alone would not suffice. I needed help on the field. I needed someone to assist me in building and preaching and raising up pastors. That's when God gave us Tom and Deanna Shaffer.

Tom was the director of radiology at Texoma Medical Center in Denison, Texas, and Deanna was a surgical assistant to a neurosurgeon in the same hospital. Having a heart for missions, they visited Mexico with us to get some "hands on" experience. On the morning we were leaving Monterrey, Mexico, we came upon an accident involving an automobile and two children on bicycles. As we hurriedly stopped, Tom ran to one injured child and Deanna ran to the other, caring for them until an ambulance arrived. This was Tom and Deanna's introduction to the mission field.

Shortly after this first visit, the Shaffers sold all they had and moved to Mexico to help in any way that they could. The first few years were spent building churches and working on the Bible school in Atoyac. During this time Tom proved himself to be a jack-of-all-trades, able to accomplish practically anything he set out to do. He was a good mechanic, electrician, plumber, builder and medic. Deanna too was an able hand in medical attention around the school and church, and she cooked a mean plate of macaroni and cheese. (If you could string up all the macaroni that Tom and I ate, it would make a necklace large enough to circle the planet!) Little did we know in those early days, the great plans God had in store for the Shaffers. Several years later we expanded our ministry to include a medical clinic in Atoyac. The clinic continues to grow, as does the medical arm of our ministry. Now we are even assisting a Christian doctor in Cuba. Tom and Deanna oversee this promising division of Mexico Ministries.

My Brother in Spiritual Arms

Russell Linscombe took the gold Rolex watch off his wrist and said, "I don't have any cash with me, but use this in the ministry." I had known his brother, Bobby, and we were having a missions dinner at the Holiday Inn in Jennings, Louisiana. Bobby had invited Russell to come and hear about the work in Mexico. He was so touched by the vision of ministry that he gave me the watch off his wrist, which I traded for money and building materials for the Bible school in Mexico. In the years since that first gift, Russell has given much more—he has given himself.

On Russell's first trip to Mexico, he, Bobby and several men from Lafayette, Louisiana, traveled just south of the Rio Grande where we built a roof for a village church. Each day the local pastor's wife and several ladies prepared lunch for us. One day they cooked up a dish of my favorite Mexican food—cabrito—young goat. When lunch was ready, Bobby and Russell were nowhere to be found. Finally, we discovered them hiding out in their motorhome dining on Vienna sausages and crackers! This was the man God was sending to help me in Mexico? Later the sausages would go, but the man would stay!

Russell and Bobby, together with a third brother Lance, and their father, Oren, have all been great blessings in my life. These four Linscombe couples have been a vital link in the strong chain of ministry God has given us.

In the early years of Russell's ministry, I wondered if he would last on the mission field. All the other missionaries I knew began their ministry under difficult circumstances. Even those appointed by a denomination had the responsibility of going out and drumming up financial support before they could "hit the field." But, Russell needed no personal support. He was blessed to have come from a financially established family and from a business that would provide income for him while he traveled on the mission field. Not only would he not take a salary from the ministry, he also contributed significant financial gifts to the work. The reason I wondered if he would last was he seemed too good to be true:

someone who loved God, longed for missionary work and was able to help in so many ways! I am happy to say he has endured and has proven to be more of a friend than I could have ever dreamed in those early days.

Russell and his lovely wife Charlotte traveled in and out of Mexico for many years before moving their family to our headquarters in Atoyac. From there he helped finish many projects while Charlotte taught English in our Bible school. Russell's ministry became a sort of combination Paul Pogue's and Tom Shaffer's work; not only would he do the hard work of hands-on missionary ministry, he would also become a contact person for introducing many others to our ministry, opening doors that no one else could. Through Russell's home church, Bethel Assembly in Lafayette, and his pastor, Mike Linney, we have been blessed in many ways at many times. Not only has Pastor Mike and the church stood by us financially and prayerfully, but they have also sent teams of men to help us with construction in Mexico. Bethel Assembly has become a pillar in the life of our ministry.

My West Texas Friends

As the work in Mexico began to expand, we found ourselves ministering to the Chamula Indians in the state of Chiapas. God began to bless the work among this tribe, and like a snowball, more congregations began to be birthed than we could keep up with. It seemed that in every village a new community of believers was birthed, and each group had a desire for a special place of worship. Arriving one day to the town of Chenahlo, I was welcomed by a long line of people flowing out from the church and down the hill toward where I was standing. Interspersed among these people were handwritten placards giving the names of their villages with the words "sin templo"—"without a church building." I pledged that day to build seven new churches, costing fifteen hundred dollars each. I didn't know how I would finance it, but I knew it was God's will.

Returning to the United States, I was invited to minister at Life Unlimited in Odessa, Texas, pastored by my good friend Don Palmer. In our time together before the service, Don and his wife Pat and I visited, but never spoke of my commitment to the Chamula Indians. Just before I was to speak, Pastor Don called me to the platform and said he wanted to present me with a special offering. Now, in my mind I was thinking, "Not now, Don! Wait until after I've preached, so the congregation can hear what I have to say." I had hoped the congregation might be able to finance one of the fifteen hundred dollar churches I had promised.

As I stepped to the platform, my friend explained to the people that God had spoken to him about an offering for our work. He reminded them that they too were involved in a building project and were believing in God for the money to build a new roof. Then he explained that God had directed him to first help build a church for Mexico, then their own needs would be met. Surp⁻isingly, he said God had even told him how much to give; and with that, he presented me with a folded check, written several days earlier. As I unfolded the check, I shouted out, from both shock and joyous excitement: the check was made out for $10,500! Exactly enough money to build the seven churches for the Chamula Indians! Don and Pat Palmer and the people of Life Unlimited, like so many other pastors and congregations throughout the United States, have served as strong team-members in our Kingdom work.

God is the Team Leader

All of these wonderful people and the wonderful things that happen through them are certainly not the result of my own endeavors or my own planning. Each person and congregation that stands with us in the spiritual battle serves to point out that God is the one in charge.

One incident that occurred in the early days of my ministry is proof of the same point: God is the real team leader. Before I had learned to communicate in Spanish, I was joined by my brother, Roger Myers, for a short trip into Mexico. We were accompanied by a couple of young Mexican men who provided us with the Spanish we needed to travel through the country. We drove down the western side of Mexico and spent several days near Acapulco, making our return through the central part of the country, through Mexico City. Having never been to "the City," I was concerned with all I had heard about its tremendous size and terrible traffic problems. I was also concerned that our traveling companions were not going to be joining us on the return trip, leaving us as helpless "English-speaking lambs" in a forest of hungry wolves.

Roger and I devised a plan that would best suit our needs: we would travel through Mexico City around midnight when the traffic would be the least. Arriving in the middle of the night we were horrified to discover that traffic never ceases in the city, and we found ourselves in the middle of a six-lane traffic jam with horns blaring and motors revving and our having no idea where we were or where we were going! After what seemed an eternity, I made it to the outside lane and exited off the nightmare. Finding an all-night restaurant, I pulled into the parking lot and just sat there trying to calm my nerves. Never did I dream, growing up on the river in south Louisiana, that someday I would find myself in such a mess!

As we sat there contemplating our next move, a well-dressed man accompanied by another gentleman left the cafe and headed our direction. I rolled down the window to attempt a request for directions, and the man walked over to our pick-up truck. Seeing my Bible on the dashboard, the man asked in perfect English, "Are you a Christian?" When I affirmed that I was indeed a believer, he asked if I were a preacher. Again, I said yes, and he replied that he too was a minister. I explained my unfortunate situation to him and told him that I hoped to reach the outskirts of Mexico City, find a motel, and get a few hours sleep before heading north the next morning. When he heard my plight he informed me that he knew exactly where I needed to go; he, in fact, lived near there, and if I would give him a ride, he would serve as my guide through the concrete jungle.

If ever I smelled a set-up it was now. But, I was desperate and helpless. I was lost in a city of twenty million, and I had found one man who spoke perfect English. I invited him into the cab of the truck while his friend hopped into the back. Our guest directed me, through many turns, to a major highway where he insisted I stop. Was it time for the robbery now? The man explained that this was close enough to his home and that I should take the highway north a few blocks to a clean hotel where we could rest. The two men got out of the truck and walked away into the night as my brother and I stared in amazement. Did this really just happen? Or was another of God's plans coming together! Farther up the road on that same return trip I again found myself lost in Monterrey. I saw a young man walking on the sidewalk so I attempted to ask directions. His response should have been no surprise by now: "Do you want directions in English or Spanish?"

When we respond to God's plan for our lives, He has a way of surrounding us with all the resources and all the people necessary to accomplish His purpose. Oftentimes such resources are found in those who become close friends and partners in ministry, but other times we find God-provided help in total strangers whom God sov-

ereignly sends our way. Either way, we find ourselves a part of a great team being used by God
to expand His Kingdom.

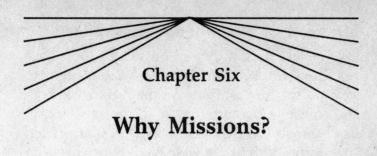

Chapter Six

Why Missions?

"Why foreign missions?"—I can't tell you how many times I've heard that question asked. While serving as a missions-minded pastor, I repeatedly had people questioning the wisdom of raising money for some foreign field when we needed money right here at home. When I answered with the principle of expansion found in Acts 1:8, "But you will receive power when the Holy Spirit comes on you, and you will be my witnesses in Jerusalem, and in all Judea and Samaria, and to the ends of the earth," many people would respond with the idea that we should take care of Jerusalem, and let someone else worry about the ends of the earth.

Later, when I responded to the call for full-time missionary service, I heard the same question asked anew: "Why foreign missions?" My parents asked the question, my in-laws, my good friends, my parishioners. "Isn't there enough work to do for God here in Texas? Doesn't our town need the gospel just as much as the far-off places?"

Missions: A Misunderstood Ministry

I believe part of the reason some people have a limited vision of ministry and are content to stay within the confines of their own territory and culture is because the very term "missionary" has been so misused. So many things are called "missions"—with such a wide discrepancy between them—that people become confused and lose sight of what true missionary work is all about.

On the one hand there are the massive crusades in the very large third-world cities where famous evangelists go in for four or five days, preach to the crowds, leave, and call it "missions." On the other hand, there are the individual ministers who pack their bags, go to a foreign field, establish a single church, pastor it for the rest of their lives, receive monthly contributions from "home"—and call it missions.

The truth of the matter is that the large campaigns are not missions in the true sense of the word. They are simply large evangelistic campaigns that happen to occur in a foreign city. They are often fruit-bearing, bringing thousands to Christ, but they are not really missionary work. The individual minister who plants and pastors a single church cannot properly be labeled a missionary either. He is simply a pastor who is pastoring somewhere outside his native territory.

A Missionary Mandate

Missionary work must have within it the apostolic elements of preaching the good news, training up local leadership, establishing churches and expanding God's Kingdom. It is a commitment to the Great Commission on a grand scale: "Therefore go and make disciples of all nations," Jesus commanded his disciples, " baptizing them in the name of the Father and of the Son and of the Holy Spirit, and teaching them to obey everything I have commanded you. And surely I am with you always, to the very end of the age" (Matt. 28:19–20).

There is then a two-fold drive behind missionary work: first, obedience to our Lord's command to go to the nations, and second, the joy of bringing the blessings of God into the lives of people who so desperately need Him. Notice the comprehensiveness of the Great Commission:

> All Authority: Jesus Christ received total authority from the Father, and in that authority commissions us to go forward with his message and his kingdom. We have all the power of heaven backing us as we respond to the call of God.

> All the World: God calls us to go into places foreign to our tastes and culture. The message of the gospel has never been a "national" message, for our people only. It transcends every cultural and national boundary and becomes a message for the entire planet. Until the entire world hears the Gospel, turns to Christ and receives the blessings of His rule, the missionary's work is not complete.

> All Truth: We are called as missionaries to do more than present the simple message of salvation. What a grand and glorious mes-

sage it is—but it is only the beginning place. We must not go in, preach salvation, and then leave the people to their own devices. Instead, we must baptize them—bring them into covenant with God, and teach them to obey all the truth that comes from the teachings of Jesus. Only then can we truthfully say we are fulfilling the Great Commission.

All Time: Christ has promised his guiding and empowering presence "always." We need not worry about going into any place at any time without the power of the Holy Spirit. What God commands, he enables. He will be with us until we accomplish his purpose— even to the very end of the age.

Ultimately, missionary work does much more than bring salvation to human souls. It transforms the individual's life. It causes the family to be whole. It changes a city. It revolutionizes an entire culture. Missionary work is the marvelous ministry of changing the world for Jesus.

An Expedition Journal

In Romans 10:14–15 the apostle Paul writes of the necessity of someone going to the people if they are to respond to God's message: "How, then, can they call on the one they have not believed in? And how can they believe in the one of whom they have not heard? And how can they hear without someone preaching to them? And how can they preach unless they are sent?" On the following pages is a short journal kept during a missionary journey into southern Mexico and

Cuba. It details the effect of being sent, going, and sharing the gospel of Jesus Christ. And, it shows the great need of missionary work that is not transient, but committed for the long-haul.

In January 1992 two traveling companions and myself took a month-long trip into the jungles of southern Mexico, and a short excursion into the nation of Cuba, scouting out new opportunities for the advancement of Christ's Church. What follows is a day-by-day journal of the trip:

January 7:

I have left my home in Denison, Texas, on perhaps one of my most challenging missionary trips. I plan to visit Atoyac and then go into the Lacandona Jungle in the state of Chiapas, Mexico.

January 8:

Visited with Moises Carranza [a leader in the Mexican church] this morning. Planned work schedule for the Hidalgo church. Arrived in San Luis Potosi about 7:30 P.M. Will sleep here tonight.

January 9:

I started my day today at 4 A.M.; arrived in Atoyac at 6:30 p.m. Good day; all went well.

January 10:

Today had been very busy. Spent most of the day with Isidro [the overseer of the Bible school and church in Atoyac] and the students. Things look well for both the church and the Bible school. We have about 20 students.

January 11:

Had breakfast with Julio [a young local businessman who is a member of the church in Atoyac]. He seems to be in better spirits. Business is better, and there have been no more threats on his life.

January 12:

Once again, I awoke at 4 A.M. to start my day. Will drive to Salina Cruz to check out that church. The road is much worse now.

January 13:

Once again up at 4. Arrived in Salina Cruz at 11. Had to make one stop to have some welding done on the trailer. Should be OK now. The church here looks good. Leave Salina Cruz at noon.

1:30: I have come only 30 or 40 miles and once again the trailer springs have broken. This time we worked on the trailer until late in the afternoon. Hope it holds together now.

Arrived in Tuxla at 9:30 P.M. Will sleep here tonight. Once again I will have to get some welding done tomorrow before I leave.

January 14:

Pastor Ayala and I leave Tuxla about 11 A.M. and arrive in San Cristobal at 12:30. Mariano has been waiting for us here. We buy machetes to take with us into the jungle.

Arrive in Palanque at 8:30 P.M. I paid for one double room for Ayala and Mariano. I will sleep in the truck to watch our things.

January 15:

We spent three hours working on the trailer before leaving. The roads were terrible. Today we have traveled 100 miles that shouldn't have taken more than three or four hours to cover. We arrived at the mouth of the Lacantum River at midnight. It had taken us 12 hours to travel 100 miles. Thank God the trailer held together!

January 16:

We entered into the river this morning and have been traveling upstream all day. This is the most beautiful river I have ever seen—the water is clear and as blue as can be. Today we saw many different kinds of parrots. As I write this tonight I am experiencing something new: we camped on a sand bar on the river and tonight I can hear the monkeys howling in the jungle—very strange sound.

I have taken no pictures yet because of rain. I have not seen the sun for several days. Today we saw many people who live along the river. Ate sardines for supper.

January 17:

It is now daybreak and I sit by a campfire on the riverbank. The monkeys have howled all night long. I am watching the parrots this morning; didn't know there were so many different kinds. Soon my two companions will awaken, and we will continue upriver; still no weather for pictures, now it's raining.

All three of us are in my tent having breakfast. I have "taken a cold" these last few days.

It's the first cold I have had in many years. I am sure that being wet all day doesn't help, but this is a rain forest, and we can't wait for it to stop raining.

The parrots are still all along the river. To-day I saw the most beautiful ones—they were as large as pheasants: red, blue and green. I also saw many monkeys—both spider monkeys and large black monkeys.

We stopped many times along the river to share the Bible, and we prayed with many. We prayed for one young boy, about 13 years old; he was sick. At one of the homes a lady gave us some beans and tortillas to take with us. We passed some men fishing in a dugout canoe, and they gave us three catfish. I cooked them tonight. We had no cornmeal, but they were good anyway. Tomorrow we continue upriver.

January 18:

This morning it is clear. From where we are camped, I can see a small village. We will stop there and share the gospel.

Today is a very special day; we met many new friends and shared the Good News. People were kind to us today. They gave us food to eat and seemed happy that we had come.

Today I had one of the rare opportunities of a lifetime. I met a man here who was born in Atoyac. He came here many years ago. After we spent some time with him he told us of a Mayan ruin that he had discovered when he first came to this area. He agreed to take

us to see it. We traveled through the thickest
jungle you could imagine, at times almost
crawling. Then we came upon a Mayan building that had never been excavated. It is not
located on any map. He told me that I was
the only outsider that had ever seen this place,
and he made me swear to secrecy. It was a
great experience.

January 19:

Today we continue upriver. We should arrive in San Andreas this afternoon.

We have arrived in San Andreas. This is as
far as we can go by boat. The river has become very narrow and very swift; there are
many rapids. From here we will go by foot to
visit a village—a small miracle! This village is
populated totally by Tzotzil Indians. Years
ago they migrated here from the home area
of Mariano, our Indian companion. He is
very excited because they all speak his language. There are approximately 200 people
in this village.

We are now sharing the Word with them.
We have been received very warmly and have
returned to the river to set up camp.

I think my cold has turned into the flu. My
body aches all over, and I can't help Ayala
and Mariano set up camp. I feel bad about
this, but they understand and are doing my
part. I couldn't ask for two better men to
travel with. Tonight they will return to the
village for service. I will remain in camp.

Two things that I appreciate very much on
this trip: my boots and my binoculars. My

boots have been very comfortable and the binoculars are of utmost benefit.

The people here are very hungry to hear the Word of God. Spent several hours this afternoon speaking to young men who stopped by our camp to talk.

January 20:

It is 6:50 A.M., and it has rained all night. Ayala has gone with two young men to check their fish nets. We have decided to stay here another day. Mariano is complaining of stomach pains this morning, and my flu remains the same. I thank God that there are people both in the United States and Mexico who are praying for us. I know that all will be well.

As the day progressed, I began to feel better. This afternoon we took a ride in a dugout canoe and shared the gospel with these people until 8 P.M.; very receptive.

January 21:

Today the rain has slowed. We will leave here and go south. Our plans are to go by boat into Guatemala; I don't know how many days that will take.

We were invited to eat with Jesus [hésōos] and his family before leaving. He fixed some chicken with thin gravy; it was good.

It is hard to leave these people. In just a few days we have become such good friends. I talked to them once again about God and then prayed for them that God would watch over them and that they would grow and mature spiritually. Part of me I leave behind.

It is now 4 in the afternoon, and we have camped on a grassy bluff overlooking the river. Tomorrow we continue south.

January 22:

Tonight we are in a small village near the Usumacinta River. We will stay here tomorrow and wash all our dirty clothes. Here we will fill the gas cans and day after tomorrow go into Guatemala by river.

January 23:

Today has been a day of rest and a day to wash clothes. I am feeling much better today, and Mariano also feels better. The sun has been shining all day. Tomorrow we will continue south.

Several people have accepted Jesus Christ as their Savior. We are now thinking of building a church for these new converts. The name of the village is Benemerito.

January 24:

We left Benemerito about 9 this morning in a hard rain. We traveled for about two hours and then stopped on the Guatemalan side of the river. There was a small house along the river. About ten of the poorest people you could imagine lived there. We were welcomed and allowed to dry by the fire. They gave us coffee, and the food they were cooking brought back good memories: catfish-head stew! After half an hour we continued downriver.

Arrived in Yachilan about the middle of the afternoon. Here are some very large Mayan ruins. The people here are very hungry for the Gospel. We shared the Word of our Lord with them until approximately 9 P.M. Tonight we sleep in the Mayan ruins.

January 25:

This morning we again shared the Word with these people for a couple of hours. They have made us promise to return and want us to bring Bibles. They fixed a lunch for us to carry with us.

Traveling on the Guatemalan side of the river, we were fired on by Guatemalan soldiers. Seven or eight shots were fired. Bullets were hitting all around the boat. Thank God we were able to cross back to the Mexican side without getting hit. I will never forget the sound of those guns. They must have thought we were part of a guerilla band; they are in constant war in this area.

January 26:

Today we had an opportunity to visit a Mayan "Lacondona" group here in the jungle. It so happened that they were having a special meeting, and the King of the Mayans was here. We were welcomed by the King, although he would not let us take a picture of him. He did let us take a picture of his son-in-law and another member of the tribe. He welcomed us to return and bring Bibles to his people.

Tonight we arrived in Palanque. I have just bathed in hot water for the first time in over two weeks. Tonight I will sleep in a bed for the first time in over two weeks. It is amazing what we take for granted in the U.S.

Tomorrow we will go to Merida where we hope to get our visas to Cuba.

January 27:

Happy birthday Ken—I wish I was at home for his birthday. Changed plans to go to Merida. Instead we arrived in Cancun at 7 P.M. Tomorrow we will fly from Cancun to Cuba.

January 28:

Arrived in Havana, Cuba, about 4 P.M. This afternoon we walked through the streets of Havana. The people seem friendly. The city looks old and in need of repair. Tomorrow, we hope to have the liberty to visit churches, if they exist. Hopefully we will also be able to visit the countryside.

January 29:

Today we spent the entire day walking the streets of Havana. This is a city of two million people; and yet, you cannot buy anything at all—not a soft drink, piece of bread, candy or anything. There are no stores to shop in. Everything is empty. We talked with several young men today. All expressed the same feelings: there is no food, the people are suffering and the young people seem very angry when speaking about the government.

January 30:

Today we hired a guide to show us around Havana. He was a very interesting young man.

His father is a member of the Communist
Party, but he himself is not. We saw a city
that, at one time, must have been one of the
most beautiful cities in the world.

This afternoon I visited an Assemblies of God
church and spoke briefly with the pastor. Even
though the conditions here are bad, the
Church is very strong. There are 90 Assembly of God churches here. They have not
been permitted to build new ones, but the
pastors said they have some 200 more congregations which meet in houses. All told,
about 10,000 believers.

January 31:

Once again, today we walked the streets of
Havana. Most of the cars here are old American cars. Many in the '20s, '30s and '40s are
still running. We talked to many people along
the streets. Times are tough: each person
gets one piece of bread per day; one egg.
The common man who has a car can only
buy two-and-a-half gallons of gas per month.

Tonight we attended services in the Assembly of God church. It is a really good church
filled with young people. I asked God to show
me why he had sent me to Cuba. I think one
reason is to somehow try to get Bibles here.
Today, we passed an old store and found
someone selling used books. He had about
twenty books and among them were three
Bibles and one paperback, "Spiritual Things."
All the books were used; one Bible did not
have a price, but the other two did: one was
$150, the other was $250; Bibles that we

would pay maybe $5 for in the U.S. The paperback book was listed at $200.

As we sat in the service seeking the full reason God had sent me here, a lady tapped Ayala on the shoulder and wanted to talk to him. They stepped outside the church and a few minutes later Ayala came back. The lady was a doctor and wanted to know if there was any way we could help with medicine. She wants to talk to us tomorrow.

February 1:

This morning the doctor came to the hotel about 7:30, and we talked until 8:30. She gave us a list of needs, and we have agreed to jointly seek a way to get medical supplies to Cuba. She said they would welcome out-of-date medicine, something the people of Mexico will not do.

I am now over the Gulf of Mexico on my way back to Cancun; we should land in about half an hour.

Arrived in Palanque at 11:30 P.M.; will sleep here tonight and continue toward Tuxla tomorrow.

February 2:

A good day. The weather was clear and we made good time driving. Arrived in Tuxla at 3 P.M. I've had a good rest this afternoon and plan to leave very early tomorrow for Atoyac.

February 3:

Started my day at 4 A.M. Left Tuxla at 4:30. Arrived in Atoyac at 6:30 P.M. Will rest here tonight and will leave at 4 A.M. heading north.

February 4:

We were up at 3 A.M. and got a little earlier start. Arrived in Monterrey at 9:30 tonight. Slow driving; it rained for the last few hours. I'll sleep here tonight and head for Texas tomorrow.

February 5:

Started at 7 this morning. Arrived home at 9 P.M. Good trip.

A Journal Postscript

Two years have gone by since this journal was written, and now I am happy to say the work in Cuba and southern Mexico has grown phenomenally. We have churches being birthed among the Indians faster than we can keep up with them, and the Cuban government has opened a wide door for us to bring Bibles and medicine into the country. Greater things are promised in the future.

Chapter Seven

When the Cause Is Greater than the Sacrifice

The letters were sent by mail to every government official in the nation: "Destroy the Jews—young and old, women and children—in one sweeping blow, destroy the Jews." The letter wasn't from Hitler, it was from Xerxes, king of the Persians in the fifth century before Christ—a king who later finds out he was himself married to a Jewish queen.

And, what was the Queen Esther to do—expose her nationality and face the threat of death, or remain silent for her own sake while thousands of her family and tribe felt the sting of the sword? It wasn't just a problem of how Xerxes would respond to the news, but there was even the difficulty of getting the news to him at all. For although Esther was the queen, even the queen couldn't just barge into the king's court without permission—such an intrusion meant an automatic death sentence unless the king himself intervened.

Esther's dilemma was resolved by the advice she received from her uncle: "Don't think you'll get through this unscathed! If you don't help rescue your people, God will raise up another, but you and your family will be destroyed. Who knows, Esther, it may be that you have been brought into Xerxes' kingdom and given this place of honor for exactly such a time as this!" At these words Esther's resolution was sure. "I will go to the king," she said, "and if I perish, I perish."

Esther had weighed the options, she had evaluated the situation, and she had come to the conclusion that this was a time in her life when the cause she stood for was greater than the sacrifice demanded of her.

Giving Your All When It's All You've Got

A number of years ago I was in a village about four hours south of Acapulco, preparing for the dedication service of a new church building. While visiting with the pastor and some American friends, someone approached me saying there was a handicapped woman wishing to speak with me. I went outside and found a young lady with her legs folded under her body, completely immobilized and sitting on the ground. I prayed with her, and after the service, gave her a ride to town so she could catch a bus to her village. She left our vehicle with a single request: "Could you please bring a wheelchair when you return?" Amazingly, I later discovered, at that very time a load of donated medical equipment was being unloaded in my garage, including three wheelchairs.

A few weeks later I returned with supplies for the school and a wheelchair for the young woman. Her pastor took me to her home, and although it was nearly dark and I was hungry, dirty and tired from a three-day drive, I was determined to deliver the gift of the chair. After making our way to the village and giving the wheelchair to the thankful woman, we began our return trip during which I began to anticipate a nice hot bath, clean clothes, a good meal, and a good night's rest.

Dropping the pastor off at his home, I was just leaving when a young man approached the van and said a sick woman in the village had requested my attention. As I considered this predicament, my body cried out, "Tired! Hungry! Need Rest! I've Done Enough Today! Enough Is Enough!" But, my spirit simply said, "Let's do it."

We drove a few blocks until the road ended, then we walked in the dark (by now it was nearly ten o'clock) until we reached a little stick and mud hut. The inside of the hut reminded me of nothing more than an Alfred Hitchcock movie set; with no electricity the room was lit by a single candle flickering from a stool in the middle of the room. In the shadows near the candle lay an old woman on a makeshift cot. She was so old and so poor and so sick. I knew immediately that she was dying, and I gently reached out and took her bony hand into mine. In a whisper she told me she had been ill for more than two years, and that for the last two months she had been vomiting blood. She had paid two witchdoctors to heal her, but they had not been successful. What was my tiredness and hunger compared to this poor creature's condition? Certainly the cause was greater than the sacrifice. I could rest and eat tomorrow. She may not be alive by then. We ministered to the woman, visited with her family, then took our leave. In the early hours of the morning, I finally made it to the motel and the bed.

A month later I passed through the same village, and the pastor insisted that I share breakfast with him. When I refused because of my busy schedule, he informed me that I simply had to stay because the meal had already been prepared with my arrival in mind. About twenty people gathered around makeshift tables as food was brought out of a house into the backyard. As we ate our meal, I noticed one of the ladies who had prepared the meal leaning against the corner of the house, arms folded, watching people enjoy her cooking. The pastor asked if I recognized her, and of course, I did not. Here was the dying old lady we had prayed for four weeks before. What a change in her now! Completely healed of the deadly sickness, her miraculous recovery had been the occasion for many in her family to come to Christ. The week before, the pastor informed me, seven of her family members had been baptized into the faith!

As I marveled at the miracle standing before me, I rejoiced that I had not refused an opportunity to minister the love of Christ to her. I had played a part in birthing a miracle! What had I sacrificed? A few hours of rest? A late dinner? But, what great gain had come because of a little obedience to the Father's will.

The Cause: The Big Picture

Taking a break from my work one evening, I turned on the television to an educational channel and found a program about the history of ancient Mexico. One segment of the program was devoted to the reign of the Aztecs who ruled in the great valley now known as Mexico City. It was pointed out that the Aztecs were polytheistic, but their primary deity was the sun god—who received human sacrifices as a means of appeasing His anger. At the dedication of the sun god's temple, the pyramid which still stands in Mexico City, more than twenty thousand human beings were sacrificed in a twenty-four-hour period. Teams of priests ripped the hearts out of living victims as the blood flowed down the sides of the pyramid steps. When one team became physically exhausted from thrusting the stone knives into the chests of their victims, another team was standing ready as replacement. The "festivities" continued for four days until the god was appeased.

When the European conquerors came to Mexico, they found this grisly tribe in power. In the name of the one true God they committed atrocities against the Aztecs that rivaled the Aztec's brutal treatment of other tribes. Within one generation of Columbus' arrival in the new world, more than 15 million Indians died as the result of war, famine, and European disease introduced by the pillagers.

The history of the people of Mexico, both Indians and Mexicans, is one of brutal suppression and ungodly poverty. To this day, many homes are nothing more than stick and mud walls with hardened dirt roofs. Village people drink the same dirty water as their animals wash in. Children sleep in cold wet beds, unprotected from the rain because of leaking roofs. Health conditions are deplorable, and the spiritual darkness over the land is immense. All the while, a wealthy elite continues to abuse the systems of power and manipulate the poor farmers and workers while growing fat on their hard labor. Witchdoctors continue plying their trade, even to the point of sacrificing human infants to appease the demons. Recently, a father and mother sacrificed their young child in order to secure blessings for their business, mixing the infant's blood with the sawdust of the floor and offering it to spirits of wickedness. Human life is cheap—babies can be had easily enough—but success in business is a rarity.

Such conditions sound medieval from another place and another time, yet this is the culture of our nearest neighbor, our "friend to the south." How deplorable, we think, and yet, what have we done to change things? Have we told them of the Father's love? Have we gone to them with the Good News of Christ? Have we shared the power of the Holy Spirit? Is the cause greater than the sacrifice?

The Cause: Some Personal Profiles

On one visit to southern Mexico I was asked to share lunch with a businessman who's life was crumbling around him. His business was bad, his family was in shambles: his wife was actually sleeping with another woman in their own home, and his young boys were growing up in chaos. As he poured his heart out, it became clear that he was at the end of his senses and had nowhere to turn.

As we ate, I gave him all the godly counsel I could and then offered up a prayer to God for him and his family. When I finished praying, he asked if I would please write that prayer down so he could take it with him and repeat it—he literally did not know how to pray. When I questioned him, he told me that he never prayed—not with his family, his wife, not over his food; he simply didn't know how. I wrote a simple prayer on a napkin and left it with him, trusting God to bless his feeble efforts.

A year later, while working on a building project in the area, I saw the man drive up in his car. He jumped out and embraced me like a long-lost loved one. Then, he told me how his life had changed. After our visit one year ago, he went home, and for the first time, he prayed at the evening meal. He continued to pray every day, and before long the woman house-guest had moved out. His wife became a Christian. Their children accepted Christ. His home, which had been so full of chaos and wickedness, was now a center for prayer and Bible study with a number of friends. He had heard that I was nearby and wanted to share his story with me.

Such is the cause in missionary work: to share Christ's love and power and see lives changed; to see hope spring forth where once despair ruled;

to see brokenness mended; to see lives made livable in the here and now, with heaven thrown in to boot.

A few years ago while driving through a small village I had worked in, I was flagged down by a woman in another automobile. When I stopped, she jumped out of her car and ran toward me, embraced me, and said how good it was to see me again. A few months before I had ministered to this young businesswoman during a time of difficulty in her life.

As we stood there she began to cry and tremble, and to increase her grip on me. I was a little embarrassed by the incident and pulled myself away from her, worried that someone would witness the exchange and misunderstand the situation. After a few minutes of talking, she calmed herself, returned to her car and drove away.

That was the last time I saw her. A short time later she placed a pistol to her head and took her own life. When I heard the news, my mind reeled and I went back in my memory to that exchange in the street. Was she reaching out to me for help? Could I have taken more time that day and made a difference? Was I more concerned with appearances than with human woundedness? What would Jesus have done? Was the cause not great enough?

To this day these questions haunt me, yet I know that Mexico is full of more people crying out for help. Young women, old men, villages, tribes are all reaching out to the Church, desperately needing what only Christ can provide. Indeed, the cause is greater than the sacrifice.

The Sacrifice

"Suppose a brother or sister is without clothes and daily food," James wrote. "If one of you says to him, 'Go, I wish you well, keep warm and well fed,' but does nothing about his physical needs, what good is it?" (James 2:15). Many see the needs around them, but few are willing to sacrifice in order to meet the needs. The Church has enough manpower and wealth to win the world for Christ. It just doesn't have enough willingness to sacrifice. Recognizing the cause is not enough. There must be a commitment to do whatever is necessary to rise to the challenge.

When Paul wrote to the Romans about the great need for evangelism he said, "How, then, can they call on the one they have not believed in? And how can they believe in the one of whom they have not heard? And how can they hear without someone preaching to them? And how can they preach unless they are sent?" (Rom. 10:14f).

There are three groups alluded to in these verses: those who need to hear, those who will go, and those who will send. We have given our attention in these last pages to those who need to hear, but how will they hear unless someone goes to them, and someone sends them.

Those who go are those who are willing to sacrifice for the sake of the Kingdom of God. Like Abraham, we are called to leave behind all

that is familiar and comfortable and follow after
God's leading into new territory we have never
surveyed before. There are frequent hardships.
There are financial difficulties. A missionary's life
is one of giving and sharing—not only from our
blessings, but from other's lack. For example, it
is possible to carry "good old American" food
onto the mission field during short excursions.
But, I could carry only enough for myself. Should
I eat what I enjoy and what is extravagant by
Indian standards, snubbing their less appetizing
fare? No. If I carried food, I would be compelled
within to share it with everyone else. We might
all get a bite, no more. So, I share not only my
blessings, but my friend's needs as well. I eat
what they eat.

On one occasion I traveled through southern
Mexico with our Bible school director, Isidro
Ramirez. We visited various pastors and enrolled
new students for our study program. Isidro had
no money, and I was paying for all our traveling
and meals. When we finally arrived to our far-
thest destination, I was nearly penniless. Isidro
wanted to continue north, and I needed to return to the school, so we counted all the money
I had left and split it down the middle. He had
enough to pay for his bus fare—but not enough
for food and lodging. I had enough to buy gasoline for a return trip, but not enough for any
extras—not even auto repair if I needed it. The
missionary's life is not his own. He belongs to
another. And, his family grows with each new
pastor, each new congregation, and each new
believer that is added to the fold.

This is not to say that the missionary life is all sacrifice and no reward. I have served as a missionary for the same number of years as I served in the pastorate, and from my experience, there is no comparison between the joys of the two; pastoring shines a dim candle next to the glory of missionary service. Of course, that is my calling, and that is where I find fulfillment in service to God.

Oftentimes the sacrifices and rewards come at nearly the same time. In January 1992, while on an expedition along the Usumacinta River that divides Mexico from Guatemala, we arrived in the river village of Yaxchilan in the middle of the afternoon. After pitching our tents in the middle of some ancient Mayan ruins, I made coffee and invited the caretaker of the ruins to sit and visit with us. After our coffee, he toured us through the magnificent ruins explaining the various buildings and their purposes.

We came upon an ancient ball park used by the Mayans in their religious sport. The guide told us the story of Mayan baseball. To appease the gods, the two ball teams engaged in an athletic competition until one would lose; the winners, being the best the tribe had to offer, would be sacrificed to the gods in a religious ceremony. The winners were taken to the top of the stone steps we sat near, were then tied to a large round stone and rolled down the steps, coming to a stop in the ball park. It was necessary, the host reminded us, to offer a very bloody sacrifice to the gods.

What an occasion to share the story of Jesus! I told the man of God's demand for blood sacrifice, and of the ultimate sacrifice made by the very best of our "tribe"—humanity. I told him how God had come among us, and Jesus Christ had given Himself on our behalf. As I shared the gospel with him, he had trouble comprehending how one single sacrifice could be sufficient for the sins of the whole world. The Mayans, he informed us, offered repeated sacrifices to the gods—shouldn't we also offer something? I shared Romans 12:1 with him: "Therefore, I urge you, brothers, in view of God's mercy, to offer your bodies as living sacrifices, holy and pleasing to God." Finally the message we were bringing began to make sense to him, and we stayed up late into the night telling him and others of the great drama of the ages. Whatever sacrifices were required for that trip down the river were certainly worth that one evening of dialogue with an old Mayan Indian. This is the reward of being a missionary. Never in sixteen years of pastoral ministry have I experienced such opportunity!

The following day we spent more time with our new friends, prayed over them, and then started upriver. It was on this day that we were repeatedly fired upon by Guatemalan soldiers. We headed for the Mexican bank of the river as fast as we could and fortunately escaped without injury. This is the sacrifice of being a missionary. Never in sixteen years of pastoral ministry have I experienced such danger!

Just as world missions could not succeed without the "goers," to be successful it must also have the support of the senders. John Donne said "No man is an island," and this is nowhere more true than in missionary work. The vast field that stands ready for harvest cannot be reaped by missionaries alone. If missionaries simply went and preached without raising up leaders, the harvest would never be reaped. But, each graduating class of a Bible college turns into twenty or thirty new native missionaries being sent out to change their world. The growth is exponential. However, such nation-changing endeavors can never be accomplished without a strong base of "senders" who stand behind the work, supply the finances for the projects, and pray for the team as it goes into the field.

In 1993 our Bible school in Atoyac had an enrollment of thirty-five students who studied and lived on campus. An additional fifteen pastors came for one week each quarter for continuing education. Every aspect of the students' education is provided for them free of charge—tuition, books, supplies, food, room—everything. Added to this expense are the monthly utilities, staff salaries, building upkeep and incidentals. Such a work is impossible for one man to do or to finance, but churches standing behind us help by sponsoring a student for a year, or purchasing textbooks or giving special offerings for the upkeep of the school. No billionaire built the school or maintains it. It is the result of real people; businessmen and children's churches, laborers and youth groups, housewives and congregations, all doing their part to raise up a future generation of spiritual leaders who will bring change to a nation in darkness.

In committing ourselves to care for the physical needs as well as the spiritual, we have established a medical clinic in Atoyac serving more than five thousand patients each year free of charge.

A single bottle of medicine can be the difference between wholeness or continued suffering. As people are faithful with small gifts, God honors it and provides a better life for the lines of people who gather before daybreak to be treated— knowing that the doctor can only treat a limited number, not because of a lack of manpower but because of a lack of medicine.

In a very real sense, missionaries are but empty conduits, ready to supply ministry from the senders to the people in need. Without the strength of supporters, the supply becomes little more than a trickle, but with committed people on the supply-end, the flow remains strong and life changing. We should never wait until we can "do something big" before we get involved in serving and giving. Churches are built, vehicles are purchased and pastors are trained because so many people are faithful not only in the large things, but in the small things as well. One tank of gasoline can be a lifesaver on the mission field; one night in a motel can give much needed rest to a tired missionary. One one-hundred-dollar bill can be the determining factor for whether a pastor's family stays dry in the coming year or lies awake through rainstorms because of insufficient covering. Every little bit matters—even a single cup of water.

Humble beginnings do not prevent these children from dreaming of a real home someday.

Chapter Eight

Culture:
A Barrier to Be Crossed

I was standing in the airport in Tuxla, Chiapas, looking out the window at a broken-down plane. Four hours late, the plane was in such bad shape that it couldn't make it from the runway to the ramp in order to unload its passengers. Three friends, American dentists, were sitting across the waiting room, patiently waiting to return home after several days of ministering to the needy Indians in Chiapas.

As we sat in that no-man's land of uncertain waiting, I struck up a conversation with three other Americans waiting to go back to New York City. We wondered aloud if the airplane was flight-worthy and spoke of how all our connecting flight schedules were long since changed. As the time whiled away, our conversation became more personal. These new acquaintances, a young couple and an older woman, were tourists, visiting the old Mayan ruins and exploring the still-primitive lifestyles of the village Indians. Our visit was congenial until they discovered my purpose for being in Chiapas. When I told them I was a missionary and that we had been in the mountains ministering to the Chamula Indians, the older woman let slip the words, "Oh no."

Here I went again! I knew I was in trouble, because only a week before I had met a retired couple from Colorado who were visiting the area and learning of the ancient history of Chiapas. They expressed to me their sadness that I was going into these pristine primitive cultures, taking away their childlike innocence and introducing them to "the Western world." When the older woman said, "Oh no," I quickly pointed out that my three friends were dentists who had been volunteering their time and talent to provide a better, healthier life for these Indians. I explained that we had been in the mountains treating poor people who had literally no other chance of receiving the kind of treatment we were giving.

"It's just a front," she replied. The real reason we were there, she said she knew, was to bring our God to them, and that to change their god was to change their culture. When I reminded her that these Indians had historically worshiped the sun, she retorted that she would rather worship the sun than the God we were trying to present.

By now her foolishness was waxing, and my patience was waning. I said, "Lady, if you knew the real Son you wouldn't be talking like that." The young man next to her threw his hands into the air, stood up and said, "I can't take any more of this." As he walked away, I wondered if perhaps I was ministering in the wrong country. It may be that our missionary work is needed more in New York City!

Isn't it interesting that people who are so concerned with preserving primitive cultures are, at the same time, very willing for changes and progressions in their own cultures. Anything that makes life easier or more pleasant is readily welcomed in places like New York, as long as places like Chiapas are kept "pure." Consider the woman I met in the airport. I guess she was between sixty-five and seventy years old, and I suppose she has lived in "the Western world" most if not all of her life. Think of the changes that have occurred in our society in the past seventy years! Yet, is she complaining about the progress of our own culture? My guess is she lives in a decent house or apartment with carpeted floors and running water. She probably has—at her finger tips—a washer and dryer, a dishwasher, a microwave oven, a television and a radio, not to mention central heat to keep her warm on those long, New York winter nights. She probably has an automobile and a garage to park it in. Add to this the access she has; anything she needs is within a twenty-minute drive from her doorsteps, including the best doctors, medicines and hospitals that money can buy.

Now, consider the Indians. Any one of them would gladly trade whatever they live in for something comparable to her garage. They have no furniture on the carpet, they have no carpet on the floor, they have no floor in the house—only the ground beneath their feet and a few sticks thrown together for a wall. The Indian women carry heavy loads of firewood over great distances in order to cook their food and warm their huts. They wash their clothes in the rivers and streams; and when they fall to illness, whether it be a cold or cancer, they simply suffer the consequences without medical attention.

However, we shouldn't do anything to change their pure and pristine culture! If their culture were pure and pristine, we wouldn't do anything to change it. But, their culture is a reflection of generations of lives lived devoid of the presence of God or His Word. These people live in a physical poverty that only reflects the poverty of their spirits. They cry out for change, for betterment, and for the hope that is found only in the person of Jesus Christ. When people talk of preserving the culture of the poor Indians, I am not convinced their motives are pure. I believe many hope for a preservation of old cultures, not for the sake of the nationals, but for the sake of the tourists. So many visitors come to view the Indians as if they were viewing wild animals in a national park, but even the wild animals are fed and cared for during the long, winter months. These Indians are not animals. They are human beings created in the image of God who deserve a hope and a future promised in God's Word.

It is true that when a people's god changes, so does their culture. But, the change is for the better. Our agenda is not to transform the Indians of Mexico into little carbon copies of Americans. They have much that is beautiful and to be treasured. Our goal is to bring them the life (and culture) transforming power of the gospel of Jesus

Christ. What needs to change in their culture will be changed for the better as God and His people show love and care for the needy. I learned in the early days of my ministry in Mexico that my job was not to make Americans, but to make believers.

A Mistaken Attempt at Changing Culture

I still remember the exact moment I learned the lesson that the missionary's goal is to change hearts, not culture. I was working in the southern part of Mexico, and being immersed in the poverty of the area, I had a great desire to change the standard of living of the pastors. Suddenly an idea occurred to me; perhaps I could transform one of the pastors, bring him into a more cultured lifestyle, and make him a shining example for all the other pastors! I carefully selected the right man and explained my idea to him. He was very much in favor of the project and eager to begin the transformation of his own personal and family life. He was, at the time, living in a run-down shack which he shared not only with his wife and children, but with an assortment of pigs and chickens that came in and out of the shack at will, and at all times of the day, including mealtimes.

With a great deal of energy and excitement, I worked hard to build a new home for the pastor and his family. After completion of the house, I supplied it with new furniture. When all was said and done, there stood a nice block home with a couple of bedrooms, a living room, a bathroom and a kitchen. It was furnished with a new living room set, dining table and chairs, beds and dresser. With great delight I moved the family into their new home and returned to the United States.

A few months later I returned to the area, anxious to visit the pastor and view his progress in adjusting to an American lifestyle. I knew the other pastors would be eagerly awaiting their own opportunities for advancement. Arriving at the pastor's home, I was welcomed into the house where we gathered into the kitchen. As we were talking around the table, I looked up in surprise as the family pig came meandering through the kitchen door. Then I noticed the chickens pecking at scraps under the table. When I walked into the bedroom, I noticed that the second drawer of the dresser was pulled half-way open, and a hen was sitting on a nest of eggs in the drawer! The pastor's wife explained to me that she thought the dresser-drawer was probably the safest place for the new chicks to hatch and grow. It was at that moment that I came to the realization that God had not called me to make Americans out of these people, but to make disciples!

As we commit ourselves to the fulfillment of the Great Commission—"Go into all the world and make disciples"—we must understand that, in the transforming of the human heart, some customs and cultural norms will change as well, but our agenda is not to change culture for the sake of cultural change. Our purpose is to bring about the spiritual transformation of the people. When their hearts are turned to God, they will abandon the wicked and perverse elements of their culture, while retaining those things that manifest their God-given uniqueness as a nation or tribe.

A Need for Human Progress

When I was about twelve years old, living along the river in south Louisiana, I enjoyed riding horses. On one occasion I came to a gate and attempted to open it without getting off the horse. As soon as the gate opened a little, the horse decided to go through. The gate-post was wrapped with barbed-wire, and as the horse squeezed its way through, the wire cut a deep gash into the top of my foot. With blood pouring from the open wound I jumped off my horse and ran to our house calling for help. My mother and father saw what had happened and immediately began applying the folk remedies of our Cajun culture. They sent my younger brother crawling under the porch to collect cobwebs, which were gathered into a handful and crammed into the open wound. The bleeding was not abated by the dirty cobwebs, so the next remedy was attempted. I was taken to the home of an elderly black woman who was known to chew tobacco. As I held my foot still, the old lady chewed a big wad of tobacco until it had reached the right consistency, then spat into my wound. The tobacco juice burned like fire, but the bleeding continued. Finally, in desperation, my parents agreed that folk remedies were not going to work, and I was taken to a distant town where a doctor cleansed the wound and stitched it closed.

How thankful I am that some customs change! When my own children injured themselves by stepping on nails or falling on rocks, not once did I apply dirty cobwebs and tobacco-saturated saliva! Instead, we took the children to the doctor, gave them tetanus shots, gave them antibiotics to fight infection, and bandaged the wounds appropriately. I suppose in a few generations even these remedies will be seen as somewhat primitive and newer, better medicines will be provided. This is only one example from an unlimited list, showing that every nation and every culture evolves. The ways of people do not remain static. Some cultures vanish, others grow and progress, but none remain changeless. When the gospel of Jesus Christ is accepted, and the Word of God is applied, it brings about blessings and progress for the people of a culture. It changes the culture for the better. God has promised "a hope and a future" to those nations who will live by His Word, and that hope and future involves a compounding of blessings so that the children and grandchildren of a people will be different from their ancestors—perhaps retaining the same language and dress and customs—but transformed by the presence of the Holy Spirit and the ethics of the Holy Scriptures.

A Twofold Ministry to Mexico

Our God-given task in Mexico is twofold: to minister to the spiritual needs and to the physical needs of the people. As we preach the gospel of Jesus Christ to those who do not know Him, we see them receiving "more life"—abundant life. But, God is not concerned with spiritual needs alone. God became flesh and dwelled among us. He sent His Son to redeem not just the human spirit, but the body as well; indeed, Christ has come to redeem all of creation! The early heresies taught that the body and the physical world were somehow evil and beyond redemption, but the Church has stood squarely against such notions by declaring that the Bible story ends with a physical resurrection of the body and a restoration of the earth and the heavens.

Knowing this truth, we cannot minister to the spiritual needs of a people and ignore their physical needs. James, the brother of our Lord, spoke of such foolishness with the example of wishing God's blessings on a hungry man but not feeding him! As we serve the spiritual and physical needs of the people, it is inevitable that some customs and culture will change, but the change is toward a godly, biblical, and blessed way of life.

Throughout my years in Mexico, I have seen so many invalids who could have been helped with proper medical attention. I have seen people permanently disabled because proper attention was not given to a broken bone, and it had been allowed to heal crooked. I have seen mentally retarded people chained to trees like animals. I have seen little children suffering from life-stealing diseases which could be treated with simple doses of medicine. These things need changing!

Recently a little three-year-old Tzolzil Indian boy was brought to us, having the worst cleft palate I have ever seen. I do not know how he had survived for three years. Unless there is immediate intervention, this human life will be lost! When a visiting American dentist saw the sad predicament of this child, he returned to the United States and served as an instrument of God to bring change to the little boy; he secured a plastic surgeon who has pledged to perform the surgery free of charge. A Lafayette, Louisiana hospital has committed to provide complimentary hospitalization, and a major airline has agreed to provide gratis transportation! What a difference godly compassion makes in the lives of the needy.

In the sixteenth chapter of Acts, Paul received a vision calling him to ministry in Europe. The vision was simply a European man saying, "Come help us." That same call goes out to Christians today; we must help those whose lives have been ravaged by the power of Satan and the consequences of generations of living without the truth of God's love and power.

That "help" may be in the form of providing Bibles and spiritual teaching, or it may be providing medicines and medical attention. Godly help can be found in something as simple as providing transportation—without automobiles it is impossible to transport building equipment, medicines, and people to the places they are most needed. I have seen as many as twenty-five people climb into the bed of a pick-up in order to avoid a five or ten-hour walk to church!

Just as Paul heard the words from the European, "Come, help us," we hear those same words from the people of Mexico and Cuba. The Indians in Chiapas, descendants of the Mayans, have been living under oppression since the days of the Spanish conquistadors. The Mexican government has shown them little attention, except to secure votes, and has, on the other hand, stripped them of their homelands and properties (much as the U.S. government did to the American Indians a century ago). Even now, innocent Indians in Chiapas are being bombed by government planes as the officials attempt to drive out leftist guerrillas hiding in the mountain villages.

While the Indians of Chiapas are being courted by radical leftist guerillas, the people of Cuba have lost their hope in leftist philosophy after enduring a generation of oppressing communism. Walking through the streets of Havana, I have had offers to purchase the clothes off my back because of the unavailability of clothing. I have witnessed the deplorable conditions of the Cuban hospitals and have heard the cry from the people, "Come, help us!" The doctors there request things as simple as pajamas for the patients and pencils and paper for the hospital offices. Any medicine is greatly appreciated in a land where nearly none exists. Can we close our ears to the cries for help? Can we say, "We mustn't interfere with their culture"? The Bible teaches us, "If a man shuts his ears to the cry of the poor, he too will cry out and not be answered" (Prov. 21:13).

Sharing Cultures

Mariano is an Indian pastor in Chiapas—one belonging to the people that my New York acquaintance insisted we should "leave alone." He and his wife sat around a campfire with a dentist friend and me as we visited together the evening before our return to the United States. Mariano thanked us for the gifts of mercy we had provided; he thanked us for the dental work that had been provided for the people; but most of all, he said, he wanted to thank us for sitting with them and talking with them, for sharing their food, their customs and their way of life.

I knew what Mariano was trying to say that night, for we had talked many times before. He had shared with me the dark history of suffering under the hand of the Spanish conquistadors. He had shown me how the Indians had been oppressed since then, by the Mexican government, and how even today they were considered, not second-rate, but fifth-rate citizens. Mariano was expressing his thanks to us that we had come among his people, not as superiors but as equals. We had slept on the same floors they slept on; we had eaten the same food. We had prayed together and studied together and worshiped together and had shared as joint heirs in Christ Jesus.

The truth is that we are not out to change culture for change's sake. We are out to expand the family of God. While we will all retain our unique and beautiful traditions, we will also grow together in the love and grace of God, recognizing one another as brothers and sisters in Christ, and children of the same God and Father of all.

Through the Eyes of the Father

During the second day of a three-day convention in Chenalho, Chiapas (the home of a new Bible school and church for the Chamula Indians), American, Mexican and Indian pastors gathered, with over a thousand Indians, atop the flat concrete roof of the school—the only place large enough to accommodate the crowd. During the time of worship, I noticed Pastor Jack Webb of Albuquerque, New Mexico, as he stood weeping in the midst of the Indians. He told me later that he had read about great revivals, but this was the first time he had witnessed such an outpouring of God's love and power.

Pastor Carlos DeCesare from Houston, Texas, was the preacher that morning, and he ended the service by asking all the American pastors to lay hands on the Mexican pastors, asking God for a fresh anointing. In turn, he directed the Mexican pastors to do the same for the Indian pastors. Then, he asked the Indian pastors to work through the large crowd and bless the Indian people. Here was demonstrated the power of the gospel to transcend all cultural barriers—Americans, Mexicans, and several different tribes of Indians joining together as the family of God. I believe God's presence was so strong that day because He was showing us that we were all His children, and He was our Father. All God's children are different, with unique customs and traditions that enrich the family of God, but beyond who we are as peoples and nations, we are first and foremost the people of God.

Chapter Nine

Looking Back, Looking Forward

Some years ago I was visiting a pastor friend who was contemplating a change in his ministry. We talked at length about where he was and where he wanted to go. My friend knew that his pastoral ministry in a particular church was ending, and he also knew where he wanted to go in his ministry. His problem was getting from point A to point B, from where he presently found himself to the place he saw in his hopes.

As I preached in his church one Sunday morning, I told the story of a man standing on a mountaintop and looking far into the distance at his destination, another peak. Separating the two mountains was a massive, uncharted valley covered with fog. The fellow had two choices: he could remain where he was and dream of the other peak or he could begin his descent, working his way through the unknown valley and step out in faith toward the goal before him. Too many people play it safe and stay where they are—never risking, never gaining. Old farmers say that a discontented cow doesn't give much milk— the same is true of ministry; without a sense of

fulfillment of purpose, we will not produce as
much for the glory of God as we might otherwise. Someone has said, "Ships are safe in the
harbor—but that isn't what ships were made for."
God doesn't call us to comfort or even necessar-
ily to safety; he calls us to service. By stepping out
of our comfort zone and into the vision that God
sets before us, we begin to truly experience a life
of faith and to find ourselves surrounded by men
like Abraham, Moses, Peter and Paul.

Looking Back

In December 1978, I stood on a mountaintop
looking into the future. I had just preached my
last sermon to a congregation I loved. The people
wanted me to remain as their pastor, but my eyes
had already caught a glimpse of a distant mountain peak. Foreign missions had invaded my heart,
and I would never again be able to put my all in
pastoral ministry. Looking forward that day, I saw
the distant mountain, but I also saw the valley
below. What if I got lost in the valley and died?
What if I never made it on the mission field?
What if their were predators down there that I
couldn't defend myself against? Should I simply
ignore the vision, let it die, and remain in the
safety of a loving congregation? Without answers,
I stepped out in faith and began journeying toward the goal. At times the traveling was difficult,
and at times I couldn't even clearly see what lay
ahead; but for fifteen years I have trekked toward
the peak, and now I see things that are wonderful
to behold.

Today I stand on the distant mountaintop. The fog has lifted, and I've even charted some new roads through the valley. My heart is fully persuaded of my calling, and I rejoice in the many adventures of faith that God has led me on during the sojourn. I glance back down the slope of the mountain and see the many churches I helped build and the many young leaders I have had a hand in training up. I see the thousands of people who have come to Christ and the thousands of patients who have had quality medical attention. Then, I lift my eyes and look back at that original mountain peak where I stood fifteen years earlier, and I give thanks to God for the courage and faith He gave me to take the first step on a marvelous journey.

It would be impossible for me to adequately cover all of the works that we have helped establish in Mexico. God has blessed us from the Texas border to the Guatemalan border, the entire length of Mexico. We have built in the deserts, and we have built in the cities. We have built small churches, we have built medium-size churches, and we have built large churches. We have built pastoral houses of all types and kinds.

The Mountain Peak at Atoyac

If you have ever driven through a range of mountains, you know that what looks like a single mountain is actually a series of peaks. A majestic mountain may have several significant peaks rising from its base. I have discovered the single mountain of my vision: ministry in foreign missions, actually has many peaks, some smaller and some very grand. In fact, with the work expanding now into Cuba and other nations, I am beginning to realize that this is not one mountain but, perhaps, an entire range! Nevertheless, thus far in my journey there have been two significant peaks that deserve recounting. They are the work in Atoyac, where our Bible school and medical clinic are located, and the work in Chiapas among the Chamula Indians and other tribes.

I first visited Atoyac with a missionary friend, Jerry McSorley, who had established several churches in the southern part of Mexico. Atoyac is located at the base of a mountain range situated about sixty miles north of Acapulco. Jerry had established a small church in the city some years earlier, and I had returned to the area a time or two assisting him in construction, staying at the home of Yayo Cejas. Well, not actually Yayo's home—a small shed behind his home. I have some lasting memories of that little shed located, as it was, so near the garbage dump. Sleep is not very restful when one contends with odor and rats! With no shower or bath available after each day's hard work, I washed in a bucket of water. Talk about a valley! How many times during this difficult season, I thought of the comforts of the mountaintop I had walked away from.

In those days I spoke very little Spanish, and Yayo spoke not a word of English except "power Jesus." Our main communication came through an old copy of *Life Magazine* that someone had given Yayo many years earlier. The magazine was in English and was filled with pictures of old movie stars. Yayo would look at the pictures and I would read the words, although he couldn't understand anything that I was saying. Every once in a while Yayo would yell out "power Jesus."

During one of those early visits, God opened to us the community of Atoyac. I had arrived only a few days after a hurricane had devastated the coastal area, sweeping into the sea many homes, automobiles and even people. The main highway leading north from Atoyac had been washed out by flooding, and a businessman friend of the local pastor invited us to survey the damage. It was about nine o'clock, and the businessman made one stop on the way to the washout to buy tacos for the workers who were laboring through the night filling sandbags used to prevent further erosion. The price of the fifty tacos came to a little under six U.S. dollars, and I asked if I could purchase them for the men. After delivering the tacos and visiting the ruined highway, we returned late that Friday evening, and I began preparing for an early Sunday return to the United States.

The following morning a local hotel proprietor named Salvador Maya sent word that he would like to visit with me. I went to his office, and he told me that word had reached him of my generosity from the night before; in fact, it seemed that most of the city had heard the strange news of an American visitor who showed concern for their problems. From the way the news had spread, you'd have thought I had built a new bridge across the washout at my own expense! Mr. Maya asked if I would be willing to speak to a group of businessmen who were meeting in his hotel, Sunday at 10:00 A.M. Since I couldn't speak Spanish, I graciously declined the offer, using as an excuse my Sunday flight out of Acapulco. The hotel owner wouldn't take no for an answer, informing me that there would be an interpreter available, and that he would personally see to it that my flight would be changed to Monday morning.

The following morning about twenty businessmen sat around tables as Mr. Maya introduced me by explaining my "generous actions" toward the people of Atoyac. Of course, this was not news to them, for word had already reached them of the kind-hearted gringo serving out tacos to road workers. The men asked many questions, and I attempted to answer them through an interpreter who knew only a little more English than I knew Spanish. Somehow we stumbled through the morning meeting, and I was kindly received by all the businessmen. Little did I know that fifty tacos would be the turning point of ministry in Atoyac! I suppose I shouldn't be too surprised because Jesus used a little fish and bread, David used five smooth stones, and Elijah used a hand-sized cloud—all to bring the blessings of God upon His people.

Impressed to hold a crusade in Atoyac, I searched out the only suitable building, a night club that held several hundred people. The owner of the club agreed to close down all activities and let me use it for one week. I invited a pastor friend from the United States to be the guest speaker, and a young missionary from central Mexico to interpret. The crusade was a marvelous success, and at its end I knew that a small church would no longer suffice as a place of worship for the large number of people who had responded to God's call on their lives.

Driving from the crusade one day, I noticed a five-acre tract of land for sale, situated on a tall hill overlooking the city. Inquiring the price, I discovered that the owners were asking ten thousand dollars. When I checked my bank balance it was zero. I was so sure this was the land of God's choice that I returned home and borrowed (against my own advice that I would give anyone else) the ten thousand dollars to purchase the property. Clearing the land by hand, in the hot, semitropical weather, I had no idea how grand the vision for that patch of ground would turn out to be. When the ground was cleared, I borrowed more money to begin the construction of a church.

I didn't know exactly what kind of building to build, but I knew that the hilltop would be a beautiful location. The hillside was filled with palm trees, and I envisioned a winding road through the palms leading to a beautiful church overlooking the city. The hill was basically solid rock, so we had to cut the ground for the foundation rather than digging it. But, we knew that whatever we built here would have endurance. This church would be, literally, a church built upon a solid rock!

The plans we designed called for a T-shaped building, with the crossbar facing the front. The crossbar of the T would be sixty feet long and thirty feet wide, and would house the classrooms and offices. The sanctuary would extend out from there, seventy feet long by forty feet wide. This promised to be the biggest building I had built to date, and also to be the greatest test of faith in raising the necessary funds. We began construction with volunteer labor and borrowed money.

After a few months of good progress on the construction of the new church, while slowly beginning to pay back the original landnote, with a few donations beginning to come in to keep us supplied with materials, I began to breathe easily again, confident that this project was going to be a success. That's when I sensed God say, "Build it two stories high, and put a Bible school in it." There went my easy breath, right out the window! I thought my faith had already been stretched to the limit, but the stretching was just beginning. I felt like the priests of Israel when they stood in the Jordan River waiting for God to provide a way across. But, I never shirked at the idea, and we went ahead with God's plans without missing a beat.

Several months later, walking in front of the church, I once again heard God's Spirit: "Build it three stories high; you're going to need it." Suddenly, I was no longer like a priest in the Jordan River, I was like Peter stepping out to walk on the water! We began the third floor the next week.

Didn't God know what He wanted done from

the beginning? Was He changing His mind that much, that frequently? Oh, but if He'd spoken to me in the beginning and said, "Build a three-story Bible school/church complex, with an additional medical clinic and dormitories for the students," I would certainly have been overwhelmed, and perhaps not even discerned such words as being the voice of God. Borrowing the first ten thousand dollars tested my faith. The total cost of the project would have staggered my mind. God only shows us what we are capable of receiving at the moment, and His revelation to us is progressive as we respond to Him in faith.

With the building completed and the school classes filled with students, we immediately found ourselves in something of a jam. The third floor was housing for the American staff. The second floor was housing for the Mexican staff and the female students, and the bottom floor was classrooms and housing for the male students. We were crowded, and every room was already used to capacity. In this situation, God spoke again and directed me to begin a medical clinic, using some of the "unavailable" rooms on the ground floor. Here we went again! This meant the financial and physical strain of building a new men's dormitory, not to mention the costs of getting a clinic up and running. But by now, I had learned to trust the voice of God, knowing that His biddings are His enablings. We built the men's dormitory, expanded the enrollment of the school, and used the lower floor of the main building as a center for medical ministry, complete with a staff doctor and Deanna Shaffer serving as assistant.

Today we rejoice over the success God has granted us in Atoyac. Our Bible school houses and trains fifty students and staff, supplying a Bible-centered education completely free of charge. Our medical clinic serves nearly seven thousand patients each year, with additional hundreds cared for in the mountains surrounding the region, again, completely free of charge. With all this success, we are not content to believe that God is finished in Atoyac. Earlier this year we began another building on the same property—a new, two-story medical clinic that will serve even more people and free up additional space for the Bible school. The new clinic will include a delivery room for new babies, an x-ray room, a surgery suite, and a dental-care room. With a two-year goal for completion, we hope to provide a place for visiting specialists from the United States to come and share their skills with the needy.

A Second Peak in Chiapas

The second peak in the visionary mountain range is in the state of Chiapas, seven hundred miles southeast of Atoyac, where a mighty revival is breaking out among the Indians of the region.

I have read of the great revivals of the past: the Great Awakening under the ministries of Jonathan Edwards and George Whitefield, the Methodist revivals with Wesley. I have been stirred by the accounts of God's work in the lives of Billy Sunday and D.L. Moody.

I have studied these great revivals, but I never imagined being part of such a grand sweeping of the Holy Spirit in my own life and ministry. But, now I am seeing an entire nation, a people, a culture, touched by God. The Chamula Indians were only four years ago classified as the "most closed to the Gospel" people in the Western Hemisphere. Completely steeped in idolatry and paganism, they have killed missionaries who have attempted to bring them God's truth, and they have driven out of their villages any converts the missionaries may have gained, burning their homes and possessions as they pushed them out of the city limits. But, suddenly God's grace is moving through the hills and valleys of the Indians, and their hearts are beginning to hunger for His presence. Four years ago, when we began working with the Indians, we had a total of four small congregations. Now there are over eighty churches, with hundreds of new converts being baptized at a time, and an unstoppable river of spiritual life flooding the land.

Those who make a commitment to Christ do so knowing it might mean total rejection from their people, but I have yet to see a single believer recant or back down from the faith. On one occasion, after spending time in various villages, our ministry team was on its way back toward the large city of San Cristobal. On our return trip we were planning to visit our church in the small village of Benisario Domingas. Running short of time and driving under extremely bad conditions, I wasn't looking forward to this side-trip; but at the insistence of our Indian pastor, Mariano, I consented to a grueling two-hour ride over dirt, rock and mud roads. Halfway there Mariano informed us that we probably wouldn't see any of the congregation, but we could at least look at the building they had built. Then he told me of the incident that had occurred there just the week before.

The Chamula Indian leaders had incited a riot against the Christians, beaten them, and then drove them from their church building. The non-believers then padlocked the church doors and told the Christians to never return for worship. The road ended at the bottom of a small hill, but what I saw on top of the hill caused my heart to leap within: a beautiful little church building built of pine boards, with over a hundred Christians gathered round the front waiting for us to arrive. As we stepped out of the truck, young people came running down the hill to greet us, taking us by the hands and escorting us to the church. Reaching the top of the hill, I saw four guitar players leading the crowd in a song: "Bienvenidos hermanos, en el nombre de Jesu Cristo"—"Welcome brothers, in the name of Jesus Christ." I wept as I walked upward to the house of God. Truly this was His holy hill.

Gathering into the packed-out building, Pastor Mariano informed the congregation that we would only stay a few minutes, owing to the jeopardy I was in as an unwelcome American in a hostile territory. As I listened to their joyous singing, I was amazed that these people who had been beaten only a week before were willing to gather in Christ's name and celebrate His goodness. I knew that our visit was important to them and that we couldn't leave after only a few short minutes. We remained for two hours, worshiped together, and enjoyed a meal prepared by the women of the church. If these people were willing to risk their lives to worship God, we as their leadership could do no less.

Before seeing us on our way, the congregation in Benisario Domingas had two requests. They wanted me to help them double the size of their church building, and they wanted to know if I would be willing to build a church in the next village if they evangelized it. I promised to help with both requests, and within a short time, we were able to purchase building material for the expansion project. Only a few months later we began building two new churches in the area— not for one newly evangelized community, but two. And, to this day, the Gospel continues to spread through these communities as people risk their all for the sake of Christ's Kingdom.

Cruston is an even more inaccessible village that can be reached only by foot or horseback. Situated high in the mountains, all the homes are made from local wood with grass roofs. We arrived by horseback in the late afternoon and pitched our tents to make camp. Joined by a number of Indian pastors who stayed in the homes of villagers, we planned to get busy the next day building a church for the newly evangelized congregation. Following an evening service in a lean-to, we arose the next morning ready to level ground for the church. However, before we could get started, a man approached the pastor saying he had a better building site that he wanted to donate to the church.

The man, who we learned was not even a member of the congregation, wanted to tear down his own home and build a church where it had stood. He asked for one week to do the demolition work and move his materials to another area of the village. We accepted his gracious offer and within two weeks had completed the new church building. I have not returned to Cruston since that time, but the church continues to thrive and reach out to the spiritually starved people of the village.

Our second Bible school is beeing built among the Chamula Indians now, and it will train up these dear people in their native language. Our plans are the same as in Atoyac: we will provide a free education to future church leaders and establish a free medical clinic to serve the sick and needy in the area. At the halfway point of building the new school, we hosted a three-day convention during which scores of pastors and thousands of Indians gathered to worship God and hear His word preached. As I looked out across the sea of people standing with upraised hands, I knew that this was only the beginning of a great move of God that will sweep the area for years to come. The believers will not number in the thousands, but in the tens of thousands. As young men graduate from school and return to their own people with the good news of Christ, we will see hundreds of churches birthed where now we see scores.

A Third and Distant Peak: Cuba

The final peak in my line of view (I should say at the present) is the island nation of Cuba. My first visit was in January 1992, and what I saw then was a nation both economically and spiritually devastated. I had ministered to the poor of the desert, the poor in large cities, and the poor in the jungle, but the Cubans were different. All the others had hope, but these people were hopeless. As I walked through the streets of Havana, I felt pangs of sorrow for the people who lived there. A city, at one time so beautiful, was not only a rotting shell, but the people who had once had such zest in their lives seemed also to be only empty shells, longing to be filled with purpose and meaning.

Since that first visit, there has been much stirring in Cuba, and it seems that not a week goes by without some Cuban story making the news. I believe that in the not-too-distant future, God will tear down the walls that surround Cuba, and there will be a great outpouring of His Holy Spirit in Havana and other cities that will rival what He is doing among the Chamula Indians now. I pray that we are positioned and ready when such a time presents itself.

Looking Forward

In retrospect, I am amazed at the wonderful things God has accomplished in our ministry, yet I know the best is yet to come. I am often asked how long I plan to work in Mexico, and I find it difficult to answer that question in terms of years. I hope to work as long as I am physically able. With God's continued strengthening, I can envision another fifteen years of labor in the field, and then I hope to spend the remainder of my life raising funds for ministry.

The work in Mexico will continue with or without me. Quality national leaders oversee the various districts of the country, and the structure there will continue to stand even if all ties to the United States are severed. Russell Linscombe and Tom Shaffer are both younger than myself, and both qualified to continue the ministry in Mexico. There are others, perhaps even unknown to us but known to God, who are standing in the wings waiting to take their place in the ongoing drama of redemption. But I love it when a plan comes together, and I am convinced that this plan of God's is just beginning to unfold!

I look forward to future projects. I hope to build a Bible school in the north of Mexico, more accessible to the border region; I see a Bible school in Cuba one day, in a country fully blessed with religious freedom. I envision additional medical services and perhaps even a stateside training center for national pastors. And, deep within my spirit, there is a yearning to go even farther south—into countries such as Guatemala and Honduras, and even Peru.

At an age when many anticipate retirement, I anticipate new challenges. I know the difference one man with a vision can make. I understand what a small team of believers working together

can accomplish. We are not alone in this task.
Christ has promised to never leave us nor forsake
us. The angels stand rejoicing in our work. What
I do with my life matters. What we all do matters.
We have a purpose to fulfill.

Chapter Ten

Where Is the Church Today?

I am often asked, where do I see the Church today, where do I see the Church going, and do I have anything to say to the Church. First I believe that we must understand that the Church is the body of Christ, as Paul writes in 1 Corinthians 12:12-13. "The body is a unit, though it is made up of many parts; and though all its parts are many, they form one body. So it is with Christ. For we were all baptized by one spirit into one body, whether Jews or Greeks, slave or free, and we were all given the one Spirit to drink." 1 Corinthians 12:27, "Now you are the body of Christ, and each one of you is a part of it." The second and equally important thing is to realize that the Church is universal. Too often our vision of the Church is too localized. If the Church that we know is doing well, then we feel that the whole body is doing well and if the Church that we know is having difficulty, then the whole body is having difficulty. We should lift up our eyes and look to the uttermost parts of the world for a clearer view of the Church, the body of Christ.

I believe that the universal body of Christ is doing well. I believe that there are areas of the world where the Church is having difficult times, some of which I will address in a few moments. But, the Church, Christianity as a whole, is stronger than ever. There are more Christians today than in the history of the world. We see the wall of communism falling and countries that have been shut to the gospel for many years are now swinging open wide their doors and inviting the gospel of good news to be preached throughout their countries. I believe that we will continue to see the gospel go forward until that Scripture found in Hebrews 10:12–13 is fulfilled: "For when this priest," speaking of Christ, "had offered for all time one sacrifice for sins, he sat down at the right hand of God. Since that time he waits for his enemies to be made his footstool." Someday this promise of the Scripture will be a reality; and I believe that a part of the body of Christ, the Church of the United States, will have much to do with the timing of its fulfillment. A great portion of God's grace has been bestowed upon the Church here in the United States and that, I believe, is for the purpose of taking the gospel to all nations.

If we, the Church of the United States, are going to help speed the fulfillment of Hebrews 10:12–13, then there are two things that we are going to have to address: first is our overzealous appetite for worldly possessions and secondly, is our willingness to hurt and destroy one another in our quest of these possessions.

Many opportunities for us to take the gospel to the four corners of the world, in this last decade, have been lost because of the overbalanced message of prosperity. We have heard quoted over and over again, for the past decade, 3 John, verse two: "Beloved, I wish above all things that you may prosper and be in health, even as your soul prospereth." We have been taught so much that God wants us to be wealthy that we have focused outward instead of inward. We have sought more, instead of sharing what we had. We have so focused on the material things that when they did not come to pass as we expected, many were too weak spiritually to face the reality; and many fell. We have heard quoted Proverbs 13:22: "And the wealth of the sinner is laid up for the just"—and many have waited and waited and waited for the windfall of finances to come rolling in. Another popular saying during this past decade was that God had signed the check and all that we had to do was just fill it out. Many churches overbuilt and many individuals overborrowed; and when it came time to pay up, and the money wasn't there, great was the fall. For the sake of privacy and the fact that I would not want to embarrass anyone, I will simply use the word friend as I share some of the destruction caused by this overbalanced teaching of prosperity.

First, let me deal with Proverbs 13:22. The Scripture says that a good man leaves an inheritance to his children's children, and the wealth of the sinner is laid up for the just. Just what is an inheritance? So many only think in terms of money. Permit me to share an experience that happened during a convention at one of our Bible schools in Mexico. Malcolm Smith, the great teacher of faith, was sharing his faith with our pastors for several days. He would teach two times a day, and my son Ken would teach one time a day. In one class that Ken was teaching, a question was asked. When were you saved? Ken responded with a question of his own. When was I lost? Now that got the attention of everyone in the house. Ken then went on to explain that, of course, he had a genuine experience and relationship with our Lord and Savior Jesus Christ. Ken explained that his great-grandmother was a godly woman and that his grandfather and grandmother were godly people and that his father and mother were godly people and that he was a fourth generation to follow that faith. He went on to explain that his earliest memories were of loving our Lord. He continued on by sharing that his three children, the fifth generation, were now walking in the faith of their ancestors. And so I say that there are some things that are more valuable to inherit than money, and one of those things is a godly heritage.

While our attention has been focused on material wealth, we have failed to see what is happening to our nation. The nation that our founding fathers established, our country, our inheritance, is being ripped apart at the seams. Everyday we hear of murders, rapes, violence—not in distant places but in our own neighborhoods. It

is no longer safe to walk the streets of our towns
after dark. Our children live with constant fear of
being molested. Gangs of youth roam our cities
and think nothing of snuffing out the lives of
others much as a hunter would take the life of an
animal. Every year dozens of innocent children
die as they are caught in the crossfire of drive-by-
shootings. And yet, the message of the last decade is that God wants to make us all million-
aires.

A few years ago, we were all shocked when a
young student climbed to the top of the tower on
the campus of the University of Texas; and from
there, with his high-powered rifle, began to take
the lives of innocent students. Since that day we
have seen so many similar acts that we are no
longer moved when someone drives up to a fast-
food restaurant and opens fire with an automatic
weapon. Life seems to be so cheap. A fan was
leaving the basketball arena in Orlando, Florida,
and en route to his car, was robbed at gun point.
When the robber realized that the man only had
twenty dollars, the robber shot his victim. He was
angered because his victim only had twenty dollars for him to rob. Violent tempers are not only
found among robbers, but all too often it is showing up in the rest of our society. Many of our
homes have become small battlefields. Battered
mothers and abused children hardly even make
the news anymore, they have become so common. Tempers flair as we crawl through the rush
hour traffic in our busy cities, and all too often
someone winds up dead on the highway because

of someone else's temper tantrum. And yet, for the last decade, so many have focused only on the message of material gain. If our nation continues to deteriorate, what good will it be to be wealthy? We had better wake up and address the more serious and important issues of life, or we may wind up like Antonio Maya of Atoyac, Mexico. Antonio became wealthy in the construction business, and not everyone was happy in the way that he conducted his business. Antonio built himself a new home and then built a twenty-foot brick wall around his house. Rarely does he leave his home. He has virtually become a prisoner in his own house. What a price to pay for wealth. Perhaps the peasant boy who has the liberty to walk the streets of Atoyac may be richer than Antonio.

A few weeks ago I sat in the office of a pastor friend who at one time had pastored a very large church whose membership numbered in the thousands. We talked about missions for about a half hour, and then our conversation focused on his ministry. He had since left his large church and was now trying to start both a new church and a new ministry. He opened his heart and shared with me, as he fought back the tears, the difficulties that he was now facing. For the first time in his ministry, he was now going door-to-door in the poor section of the city, inviting the people to come to his church. He said, "I don't know how to relate to the poor." He said that all of his ministry, he had surrounded himself with the elite of his area and that now he was having to learn what it means to have compassion for the needy.

We prayed together that day, and as I was leaving, I thought how wonderful it would have been if only my friend had found compassion for the poor and needy earlier in his ministry. What a difference it might have been.

There is another aspect of the overbalanced message of prosperity. In our desire to believe that each new day would hold the answers to our financial needs and desires, many new ventures were entered into, ill-advised. New businesses, new homes, and new church buildings were being erected at an alarming rate, and many of them were on the premise that tomorrow there would be rivers of finance flowing into our lives.

Churches with congregations of two to three hundred members were suddenly building new sanctuaries that would double and sometimes triple their monthly operating expenses, thinking all the time that there would be an abundance of money to cover all costs. Many churches became overstaffed with new, paid positions that the church had never experienced before. There was the pastor, associate pastor and their secretaries. Then there were the pastors of music, education, men, women, youth, children; and each of these departments had their own secretaries, and everybody was drawing a nice salary. Hardly anyone was volunteering to do anything—after all, there would be enough money to pay for everything. We had crossed over into the land of milk and honey. We had entered into Canaan land; and then, reality began to set in. We realized that today was no different than yesterday and that

tomorrow would be much like today. Our towers
of Babel began to crumble, and great was the fall.

I think of my young pastor friend who is now
struggling to keep his congregation together. A
few years ago my friend found himself in an
awkward situation. He stood behind the pulpit
and looked out across the spacious new audito-
rium and into the faces of a congregation who
were wondering what had gone wrong. It was
now approximately two years since the church,
like so many others, had built a new building. At
the time of the building, my young friend was
youth pastor; and now, he stood behind the pulpit as senior pastor of the church. It seems that
when the financial crunch hit, many of the congregation jumped ship. This made a difficult situation even more difficult. Now it would be even
harder to meet the monthly expenses. Because of
the mounting pressures, the senior pastor had
left the church, and the remaining congregation
had turned to the youth pastor for their spiritual
guidance. My friend did the only thing that he
could do with a small congregation and a large
financial load—sell the building and start all over
again. The congregation now meets in a store
front in a strip-mall. Another lesson had been
learned, the hard way.

Please do not misunderstand me. I want to
make it very clear that I am not totally against
prosperity or the message of prosperity. I believe
that it is biblical and that the peoples of the world
should hear it and know that our heavenly Father
is concerned about His own. I just believe that it

should be presented in it's proper context and in a balanced way as the Bible teaches prosperity. Daily I am experiencing the fulfillment of 3 John, verse two. My health is good, and my relationship with our Lord is good, and all of my personal needs are being met. Not only am I blessed, but we are also experiencing the same blessing on the mission field. I believe that as we seek to fulfill His commandments—all of them—then all of our needs will be met according to His Word in Philippians 4:19: "And my God shall meet all your needs according to his glorious riches in Christ Jesus." Speaking of our daily needs, Jesus Himself said in Matthew 6:33, "But seek ye first the kingdom of God, and his righteousness, and all these things shall be added unto you."

Perhaps, I can sum up how I feel, and how I believe that our Lord feels about this subject, by sharing with you an illustrated sermon that I preached some while back. I took my text from Luke 16:19: "There was a rich man who was dressed in purple and fine linen and lived in luxury every day. At his gate was laid a beggar named Lazarus, covered with sores and longing to eat what fell from the rich man's table. Even the dogs came and licked his sores." I titled my sermon, "The Man in Purple."

Prior to the service, a table was placed on one side of the platform and covered with a linen table cloth. On the table was placed a candle, a couple of wine glasses, place settings for two, and a loaf of bread. There were also two chairs, one on each side of the table. As I read my text and began to speak, a young man entered into the church and began to walk down the aisle toward the platform. He was dressed in very fine cloths and was wearing a purple robe. As the congregation—unaware of what was happening—looked on, the young man made his way to the platform; after pulling out a chair, he sat down at the table. I continued to speak and a few minutes later another young man entered into the back of the church, and he too began to make his way down the aisle toward the platform. This young man was dressed in tattered, dirty clothes and really looked like a bum. He made his way to the opposite side of the platform and, reaching the first step, sat down. Now, I was ready to begin, in earnest, my message.

First, I dealt with the man in purple. The Scripture says that he lived in luxury every day. I imagined him to live in a very nice home, perhaps sitting off the road a short distance, just far enough to keep the dust from passing horses and chariots from settling on his home. I pictured his house with a nice front porch facing the road where he could sit and watch the people going to and fro. There would be a table on the porch and always with food and drink at his command. He would also have servants to wait upon his every desire. In reality, I guess that you could say that he had need of nothing.

Down the lane, at the entry of the rich man's property lay a poor man. They called him a beggar. He is believed to have been crippled and unable to walk. It is thought that he had to be carried to the rich man's gate, where he would beg for help to sustain his life from day to day. The Scripture says that his body was covered with open sores that the dogs would lick. He would look down the lane to where the rich man was feasting and wished for the crumbs that fell from the rich man's table, but to no avail.

My first question to the congregation was that if these two men represented life today, those who have and those who have not, then to which should we be preaching the gospel? Their response was that both needed to hear the gospel, and they were right. My second question was, to whom are we preaching the gospel? During this last decade, much of our time was spent telling the man in purple just how important he was. Our sermons were addressed to him and rarely did we look down the lane, near the gate where lay the beggar. Our churches were built to better serve the man in purple, and our books were written for his benefits. I doubt if the beggar could even read, and if he could, he didn't have the money to buy a book.

My final question was, what would Jesus do? I then turned and sat down in a chair on the platform. As I sat down, the song "What Would Jesus Do?" was sung. About halfway through the song, the man in purple rose from his chair and walked across the platform to where the beggar lay on the platform step. He reached down and took the beggar's hand and lifted him to his feet. He embraced the beggar for a moment and then led him across the platform to the table. They stood there together, and then the rich man took off his purple robe and placed it upon the beggar. He pulled out the chair and seated the beggar at his table. Suddenly, the congregation saw the full picture and they rose to their feet and applauded. Many of them wept as they realized that is not only what Jesus would do but that is exactly what he did do. He left the banquet room of heaven and came in search of you and me, the beggars; and when He found us, He clothed us in His righteousness and invited us to dine with Him throughout eternity.

Chapter Eleven

War in the Heavens

As I went to the mission field, I knew some of the obstacles that I would be facing. I knew that there would be the financial obstacle, and I knew that there would be the language barrier. There would be another obstacle that I was totally unaware of and, for the most part, unprepared for. It was spiritual warfare. Though I had studied it and thought that I knew somewhat about spiritual warfare, I would soon find out, to know a little bit about it and to be involved in it are totally different.

Daniel understood spiritual warfare. He writes in Daniel 10:10–14:

> A hand touched me and set me trembling on my hands and knees. He said, Daniel, you who are highly esteemed, consider carefully the words I am about to speak to you, and stand up, for I have been sent to you. And when he said this to me, I stood up trembling. Then he continued, do not be afraid, Daniel. Since the first day that you set your mind to gain understanding and to humble yourself before your God, your words were heard, and I have come in response to them.

But the prince of the Persian kingdom re-
sisted me twenty-one days. Then Michael, one
of the chief princes, came to help me, because I was detained there with the king of
Persia. Now I have come to explain to you
what will happen to your people in the future, for the vision concerns a time yet to
come.

The apostle Paul understood spiritual warfare.
Paul writes in Ephesians 6:12, "For our struggle
is not against flesh and blood, but against the
rulers, against the authorities, against the powers
of this dark world and against the spiritual forces
of evil in the heavenly realms." The apostle Paul
also writes in 1 Thessalonians 2:17–18, "But, brothers, when we were torn away from you for a short
time, in person, not in thought, out of our intense longing we made every effort to see you.
For we wanted to come to you—certainly I, Paul,
did, again and again—but Satan stopped us."

Our Lord Jesus Christ knows what spiritual
warfare is. In Luke, chapter four, Christ speaks
of His encounter with Satan after His forty-day
fast. And, He explains to Simon Peter, Satan's
desire to destroy Him, in Luke 4:31, "And the
Lord said, Simon, Simon, Satan has asked to sift
you as wheat. But I have prayed for you, Simon,
that your faith may not fail. And when you have
turned back, strengthen your brothers."

Perhaps the greatest example of spiritual warfare that I have ever witnessed was in Atoyac,
Mexico. For several nights, we had been having
special services in our church. People would leave

their homes in the afternoon and walk to church. Some of them had to walk several hours to reach the church. Each night, after the service, various ones who owned automobiles would take the people back to their villages. I had been using my van to take a small group to a village some four or five miles away. On the last night of our meeting, I would not be able to help this group because we had several friends from the United States visiting, and I would have to take them back to their hotels in Acapulco, about a one-hour drive. Prior to the service, I asked Arturo, a young man in our church if he would help me out and take the people to their village. Arturo agreed to help me.

We had a great service that night, and as the service was ending, the congregation stood and we were closing our service with singing and worship. I noticed Arturo, who had been sitting in the front row, was now standing and worshiping our Lord Jesus Christ. Within a few moments, I saw a complete change come over Arturo. In the beginning, his hands were lifted in praise, and there was a countenance of joy on his face. Now, his hands were down by his side swinging to and fro. His worship turned from praise to travail. Swinging his hands back and forth, he bowed lower and lower toward the floor and the travailing of his spirit became more intense. I had never witnessed anything quite like this in all of my ministry, either in the United States or in Mexico. Although I did not know exactly what was happening, I did know that there was a seri-

ous spiritual battle going on. I felt that Arturo's
very life was in the balance. I stepped from the
platform and walked over to him and put my arm
around him and also began to pray. I asked God
to spare his life. Within a few minutes, a peace
returned to Arturo.

Our service ended; I took my American friends
to Acapulco, and Arturo took our Mexican friends
to their village. I returned to Atoyac about one
o'clock in the morning. At about nine o'clock the
next morning, we were having coffee when Arturo
walked in. He looked bad. His clothes were soiled
and torn, and his hair was matted with dirt and
leaves. Arturo sat down and began to tell us what
had happened.

He had crossed a little river to get to the
village where he was taking the church members.
After the people had gotten out of his truck, as
he was returning to Atoyac, reaching the river, he
was stopped at gunpoint by three armed men.
Arturo was kidnapped, bound with a rope, his
own shirt used to blindfold him, and he was placed
in the back of the truck. One of the kidnappers
drove Arturo's truck, and they took him on a
drive up into the mountains for several hours.
There they tied him to a tree, and after a half-
hour of talking, they decided that they would kill
Arturo. He said that he began to plead for his
life, begging them not to kill him. One of the
men said that their boss said that he must die
because he knew who they were. Arturo continued pleading for his life, saying that he had a
little three-year-old girl and that she needed him

alive. After some time of talking, the men left him and walked over near to where they had parked the truck. Arturo could hear them, but he could not understand what they were saying. Once again they returned saying that he must die. Again he pleaded saying, "I have a little girl, and she will need me." The men walked away, and he heard his truck start up and leave. Some time passed, he was not sure exactly how much, perhaps an hour or two, and then he heard his truck return. One of the men approached Arturo and said that the boss said that he must die because he knew who they were. Again, his only plea was that he had a little girl and that she would need him alive. The man who was talking to him left, and he heard them drive away in his truck. This time they did not return. Sometime before daybreak, Arturo was able to free himself and walk down the mountain until he came to a road where he caught a ride back to Atoyac.

Now, I ask you, was it Arturo's ability to plead that saved his life? Was it the fact that he had a little three-year-old girl at home who needed him? Did the man that he was pleading with also have a small girl and, perhaps, was moved with compassion? My answer would be, none of the above. I believe that the battle was won the night before in the church service. I believe that the angels themselves joined in prayer with Arturo, and the Spirit prayed through his as we read in Romans 8:26, "In the same way, the Spirit helps us in our weakness. We do not know what we ought to pray for, but the Spirit himself intercedes for us with groans that words cannot express."

A few months went by, and as was his custom, about nine o'clock one night, Arturo went to his business to check and make sure that everything was secure. As he opened the gate to enter, he saw a man standing only a few yards away with a pistol raised and ready to fire. Arturo raised his arm as if to block the bullet. The first bullet hit him in the arm, and he fell to the ground. He started to get up and the second bullet entered his right shoulder and exited beneath his left ear. It had traveled through his neck without hitting the spinal cord or a bone in his neck. As Arturo lay on the ground turning and twisting, the gunman continued firing until his gun was empty. Arturo then got up and ran across and down the road until he came to a little restaurant. An ambulance was called, and Arturo was rushed to a hospital in Acapulco. Arturo fully recovered from his wounds.

Now, once again I ask you, why was Arturo's life spared? Was it because he is an extraordinary person? One that even bullets cannot hurt? Was it that the gunman was a bad shot as he emptied his revolver as Arturo lay twisting on the ground? Or, was it that the battle for his life was decided on that last night of services in our church?

Much has been said and written about spiritual warfare. Some believe in spiritual warfare, and others do not. But, when you see something so real happen before your very own eyes that defies natural reason, then it becomes much easier to believe.

As I travel from village to village throughout

the mountains of the state of Chiapas, visiting the various tribes of Indians, I see the evidence of a battle far greater than the physical. On the one hand, I see a simple, yet kind and gentle people. I see a people who want to be helped and are crying out, "help us"—a people who are so hungry to hear the gospel of our Lord and Savior Jesus Christ—a people who are willing to walk for hours just to hear the gospel preached. On the other hand, I see a people, even in this modern day, who are suffering as if this were ancient times—a people who are dying of curable diseases. I see the small children with swollen stomachs, and I know that they are full of worms. Almost without exception, all of the children constantly are with colds. They cough and their noses run because of the congestion. I have gone into their houses of sticks and mud and seen where they sleep on the ground. I have prayed with them in their homes as they lay sick with fever. Oh, how I have wished for some of the simple medicines that we so take for granted here in the United States. Things such as cough syrup, vitamins, tylenol or other medicines that would help give relief from the pain.

I see all of this and I wonder aloud: God, what a battle that must be being waged in the heavens over the destiny of these precious souls. I read in John 10:10: "The thief comes only to steal and kill and destroy; I have come that they may have life, and have it to the full." Here are two visions for the lives of these Indians: God's vision—to give them life and that to the fullest, to bless them, to lift them up and give them a better way of life. Satan's vision is to rob, to kill and to destroy—not only to keep them from being blessed and their standard of life bettered, but also to take from them what little they do have. These two visions, as giant thunderstorms, do clash in the heavens in a spiritual war: good against evil, angels against demons, with the destiny of these people at stake.

Satan has always had a vision of hurt and destruction for the Indians. For hundreds of years he watched with pleasure as they offered up human sacrifices unto pagan gods. How Satan must have gloated when in a four-day period, over twenty thousand human hearts were ripped from the bodies of the Indians and offered to the sun god. That was his desire: rob, kill and destroy. When the Spanish came and Satan's domain was threatened, he altered his plan, but his vision remained the same. He placed within the minds of the Spanish, the thought that the Indians were pagan animals fit for nothing but to be destroyed, and in fifty years, over fifteen million Indians died. Many were slaughtered like animals—men, women and little children. And now, once again Satan's domain is threatened. This time it is with the gospel, the good news, the pure Word of God. Satan knows that if they hear, they will believe; and that if they believe, they will be saved; and that if they are saved, they will have access to the heavenly Father through Jesus Christ, and their lives will be changed forever. Through prayer and worship and the Word of God, they will have life and that to the fullest. So how will he stop them from hearing and believing. Stop the ones who bring to them the gospel. It worked in Jerusalem, so why not in Chiapas. "O Jerusalem, Jerusalem, you who kill the prophets and stone those sent to you . . ." (Matt. 23:37).

It was 25 January 1992, about the middle of the morning when I heard a loud pop and stopped the outboard motor to see what had happened. For several weeks we had shared the gospel with the Indians who lived along the rivers. Now I was approaching a group of people standing on the bluff overlooking the river. I was about fifty yards from the group when I felt a check in my spirit and turned the boat from the Guatemalan side of the river and headed toward the Mexican side. Hearing the loud pop and stopping the motor, I asked my traveling companion, Pastor Ayala, what was the noise? He said that we were being fired on by Guatemalan soldiers. I restarted the motor and as the bullets ripped through the water all around the boat, I headed toward the Mexican side. They continued to fire at us until we had completely crossed the river. Satan said, "I will stop the one who carries the gospel"; and God said, "Not today," and He covered us with His hand and His grace was sufficient.

On another occasion, I had flown into Tuxtla, Chiapas, and was met at the airport by Carlos, a young Mexican pastor. With Carlos was one of our Indian pastors, Pastor Marcos. The three of us got into the cab of the pickup and headed into the mountains where we would work several weeks with the Indians. Carlos was driving, and I was in the middle, and Marcos was on the passenger side. We had been driving for about an hour and were now at about five thousand feet elevation. It was raining lightly, and we were going around hairpin curves when Carlos asked me how was his driving? I said just fine. He said, "Good, I've only been driving for about eight months." My heart skipped a beat, or to be honest, several beats. Within five minutes, Carlos lost control of the pickup, and it turned completely around in the road and began to slide off the mountainside. Would this be the day that Satan would succeed? Would this be the day that he would stop the gospel from reaching the Indians, at least through my ministry. It is surprising how many things can pass through your mind so quickly. Only a few weeds stood between us and a several-hundred-foot fall. As the truck began to slide off the mountain, it struck something in the weeds and stopped. The right front wheel of the pickup was hanging over the side of the mountain and spinning freely in the air. We carefully got out of the truck, hoping that it would remain balanced and not fall. Then we found out what we had hit. It was a big rock that had been dislodged from the mountainside during the rain and had rolled across the road and lodged in the weeds. And now I ask you, who put the rock in the weeds? Satan said, "I will stop the one who carries the gospel," and God said, "Not today."

And so, the war continues on, spirit against Spirit—and I am caught in the midst of it. Because of this, I realize the importance of prayer; I covet the prayers of believers. There are many other experiences that I could share. Times when traveling at night, I would have been robbed by bandits who had set up road blocks, but I somehow found a way to get through. There were times of traveling many days and nights with very little sleep, and yet instead of being tired, I would find a strength almost superhuman, and I knew that someone was praying for me. Somebody was touching God in my behalf. Spiritual warfare, is it real or just imaginary?

Shown here in native dress are young Tzotzil Indian men who will spread the gospel among their people.

Chapter Twelve

And the Poor
Also Preach the Gospel

I sometimes feel like David must have felt when he fled to the cave of Adullam, in 1 Samuel 22:2: "All those who were in distress or in debt or discontented gathered around him, and he became their leader." Unlike King Nebuchadnezzar, who was able to select the very best, the brightest minds (when he selected Daniel and his friends), David had to settle for a ragtag bunch of discontents. But with this group, David would win great victories for the Kingdom of God. Sometimes I look at our group and wonder: how is it that we can do anything for the Kingdom of God? And then, God reminds me that it is His grace that is sufficient.

Heber Ayala is one of those whom God has placed in our lives and ministry. I am not so sure that Ayala would have fit into David's army. The Scripture says that the men who came to David were in distress, in debt, and discontented. Now Ayala would have qualified in all of these ways, but what might have bothered David would have been the other circumstances of Ayala's life. You see, the first half of Ayala's life was a life of sin—

Sin with a capital *S*. He was a drug dealer in the country of Mexico. He both bought and sold all types of drugs. Not only did he deal in drugs, but he also used drugs. He used marijuana, cocaine and heroin. He joined a drug gang and began to traffic drugs into the United States, mostly through Tijuana, Mexico, into San Diego, and up the coast of California.

During his drug years, Ayala suffered much. He was cut with knives in fights. He was shot twice and served time in prison, both in Mexico and in the federal prison in Lombard, California. It was while he was serving time in the prison in the United States, that someone gave him a New Testament. Through the reading of the New Testament, he developed a hunger to know more about God. Upon being released from the prison, he immediately began attending church and within a short time found himself desiring to become a minister. After several years of working with his pastor in the United States, he decided to return to Mexico and preach the gospel. He sold all that he had and moved his family to the state of Chiapas and began preaching. When God brought our lives together, Ayala was pastoring a church that was half-built and four small missions in the mountains with the Tzolzil Indians. From that day on God mightily blessed, and today we have over eighty churches in the state of Chiapas and Pastor Ayala is general pastor over the entire district. Misfits in the hands of society often become great fits in the hands of God.

During the last five years, Pastor Ayala has

been my right arm in the southern part of Mexico. He has accompanied me on many journeys throughout Chiapas. Together we have crossed over mountains on horseback to reach the remotest villages. We have traveled by river through the jungles of southern Chiapas. We have walked the streets of Havana, Cuba, together. He has been to me what Luke must have been to the apostle Paul. In the midst of danger, he has stood firm; never once has he weakened or turned to run. Because of this man, the Kingdom of God continues to be blessed.

Another who would have had qualifications to join David, is Jonas Garcia. Most of Jonas' ministry has been as an evangelist. His evangelism ministry carried him to the state of Sonora, just south of Arizona. There he established a few small missions. Each time that I would see Jonas, he would ask me to come out to his area and see what he was doing. His area was so far out to the west that it would be very difficult for us to take groups out to help him, so we asked if maybe it might be better to turn over his works there to some missionary in the state of Arizona. He could then move back a little closer to where most of our works were. The next time I saw Jonas, he told me that he was working in Monclova, Coahuila, Mexico. I was glad, for it would be much easier to take groups from Texas into Monclova to help him in any works that he might establish.

About a year would pass before I would see Jonas again. He had come to our Bible school in

Atoyac for a district meeting. I asked how his ministry was going and he said, come and see. I promised that I would as soon as time would permit. In the early part of 1994, a group of friends from Texas joined me, and we went to Monclova to see what Jonas was doing. What I saw was very pleasing. There was one concrete block building, about a twenty by twenty feet square. There was also another structure that was partially started. This would be the beginning dormitories that would eventually house approximately forty people. They were also digging the footing where they hoped to someday build a church. As pleasing as it was to see what he had done, what I was to hear would be even more pleasing. He called his work, "La casa de refugio," the house of refuge.

Pastor Jonas told of how he began the work in a borrowed, two-room house with only a foam-rubber mattress, one drinking glass, and one kitchen knife. He went into the streets and preached to the street people. The drug addicts, the alcoholics, the prostitutes—any who would hear his message. He said that there were now twenty-seven living with him in that one small room that they had managed to build with donated materials. And then, Pastor Jonas began to introduce us to several of those who were living in the house of refuge.

There was Juan Reyes, who told us that he was an alcoholic for seventeen years. He was living in a cardboard box in the city park when Pastor Jonas first saw him. He said that it had

now been seven months since he had taken a
drink. Not only had his life been rescued and
turned around, but now he too was going out
into the streets to tell the good news, that Jesus
Christ does care and does make a difference.

We heard Enrique Peralta give his testimony.
Enrique and a young man by the name of Jesus,
who was also at the house of refuge, had both
served time in the same prison, at the same time,
for the same reason. Both were dealing in drugs.
Upon being released from prison, Jesus had
turned to the house of refuge for help, and his
life quickly turned around. Enrique too was released, but went back to selling and using drugs.
He said that because of his life of sin, he had lost
all that he had—even his wife and three children.
He said that one day he saw Jesus on that street
and went up to him to sell him drugs. Jesus told
him that he did not need them anymore, that he
had found the Lord Jesus Christ and that he was
living a new life. Enrique said that he looked at
Jesus that day and remembered their time in
prison. He said that in prison, he was the macho
one and Jesus was the meek one; but he said that
day he saw something in Jesus that he himself did
not have, and he wanted it. He said, he came to
the house of refuge and found Christ, and then
he began to cry. Then I saw three small boys walk
up to him and stand by his side. They were his
children; they too were now living at the house of
refuge. Enrique was not the only one crying. I
saw grown men, American men, wipe the tears
from their eyes.

And then there was Alfredo. The first words that he said were, they called me crazy. He went on to share with us his life of fourteen years, living on the streets as a lunatic—sleeping on the streets and eating out of the garbage cans. He said that he was twice hospitalized for insanity, put on heavy medications and given shock treatments. He too was reached by someone from the house of refuge, and now his desire was to return to the streets, but not to live: this time it would be to share his testimony of a life changing experience with Jesus Christ.

We bought cement, steel, sand and gravel; and our friends from the United States joined the new converts, and we worked together for a week. Even though we had worked together on other mission trips, this one seemed a little different, a little more special. It was as though we were seeing Matthew 25:34–40, come alive:

> Then the King will say to those on his right, Come, you who are blessed by my Father. Take your inheritance, the kingdom prepared for you since the creation of the world. For I was hungry and you gave me something to eat, I was thirsty and you gave me something to drink, I was a stranger and you invited me in. I needed clothes and you clothed me, I was sick and you looked after me, I was in prison and you came to visit me. Then the righteous will answer him, Lord, when did we see you hungry and feed you, or thirsty and give you something to drink? When did we see you a stranger and invite you in, or needing clothes and clothe you? When did

we see you sick or in prison and go to visit you? The king will reply, I tell you the truth, whatever you did for one of the least of these brothers of mine, you did it for me.

Chapter Thirteen

Love Can Build a Bridge

The apostle Paul begins the thirteenth chapter of 1 Corinthians:

> If I speak in the tongues of men and of angels, but have not love, I am only a resounding gong or a clanging cymbal. If I have the gift of prophecy and can fathom all mysteries and all knowledge, and if I have a faith that can move mountains, but have not love, I am nothing. If I give all I possess to the poor and surrender my body to the flames, but have not love, I gain nothing.

Paul continues,

> Love is patient, love is kind. It does not envy, it does not boast, it is not proud. It is not rude, it is not self-seeking, it is not easily angered, it keeps no record of wrongs. Love does not delight in evil but rejoices with the truth. It always protects, always trusts, always hopes, always perseveres.

The apostle Paul closes chapter 13 with these words: "And now these three remain; faith, hope and love. But the greatest of these is love."

The Judds of country music fame, produced

both a song and video entitled, "Love Can Build
a Bridge." In their song were these words: "Love
can build a bridge, don't you think it's time, don't
you think it's time?" Not only is it time, but it is
past time. We have been separated too long.
Separated by racial barriers, economic barriers,
denominational barriers, political barriers—barriers that can and need to be bridged, and love can
build that bridge. Don't you think it's time?

I remember many years ago, my younger
brother Dean and I had gone to check the trout
lines in the Mississippi River. Dean and I were
both in our early teens. It was late in the afternoon when we crossed the river to run and bait
our trout lines. We were just beginning to run
our last trout line when I looked to the north and
saw the storm coming. The sky was blackening
and lightning was flashing, and the storm was
coming very fast. We would have to cross back
over the Mississippi River, but I did not want to
leave without baiting the trout line. I determined
to bait until the last moment; and as the winds
would hit, I would drop the line, start the motor
and cross the river before the waves would have
time to build. The winds hit. I dropped the line
and grabbed the pull rope to start the outboard
motor, but it would not start. I frantically pulled
again and again but to no avail. By now we were
two very scared young boys. What should we do—
stay the night in the woods along the banks of
the river, without shelter, wet and cold; or should
we try to cross the river without a motor, a river
that was now churning with white-capped waves?

The decision was made. I knelt in the front of the small, flat-bottom jon-boat and began to paddle across the river, a river that was at least a half-mile wide. I thrust the paddle deep into the river and pulled hard, again, and again, and again. The hard current aided by the strong wind was sweeping us down-river at a rapid rate. The waves were now breaking over the sides of the boat. Added to our fear of sinking was also the fear that one of the many tug boats that push their long strings of barges up and down the river would not see us and run over us. With all of my strength, I paddled, while Dean frantically bailed out water. As we reached halfway across the river, I could see my dad standing on the river bank waving to us. He had seen the storm building and had come to help. But, what could he do? There was a quarter of a mile of raging river between a worried father and his two sons. Oh, if only there would have been a bridge—a bridge that would have let us go to him or him to us.

By the grace of God, we made it across the river that day. But, I wonder how many thousands of others there are today who are at the point of drowning in the middle of the rivers of life. And, they too cry out. Oh, if only there was a bridge. There can be a bridge. There will be a bridge. There is a bridge being built today, and it is a bridge of love. Love can build a bridge; and yes, it is time.

We are joined by a number of pastors from Church On The Rock, International—pastors who are helping to build a bridge from the United

States to Mexico, even to the most remote areas of Chiapas where the most primitive dwell. They are pastors who are not so concerned about naming the bridge as they are about building the bridge—pastors who have been there. They have seen the hungry (both spiritually and physically). They have heard the cry for help and they have responded to the cry with help.

We are joined by independent pastors, such as Lee Lamury, Don Palmer, and others who are concerned with building not only a bridge which reaches from the United States to Mexico, but more importantly, one that reached from heaven to earth, from God to man.

We are joined by Baptist, Assemblies of God, Christian, Church of God, nondenominational, and Catholic churches who realize that love can build a bridge and also realize that that bridge is long overdue. We need more men—like Bishop Dale Howard who pastors the Church of the Messiah, a charismatic Episcopal church in Jacksonville, Florida—who believe that the Kingdom of God is more important than the kingdom of man.

We are joined by individuals, old, young, white collar, blue collar, poor, rich, professional, common, men, women, and children—all who believe that together we can build a bridge. Doctors like Tom Watson and Don Middleton not only are willing to share their professional abilities but are also willing to roll up their sleeves and mix concrete or whatever is needed to be done. Dentists like Carl Breaux, Jim Nichols, and Jerome Smith donate their time, pay their own expenses and travel to the most remote areas year after year, just to help the needy. Children like Andria, a ten-year-old girl who sends an offering to a little Tzolzil Indian girl; children, like the group from Calvary Temple in Baytown, Texas, who raised enough money to build a church for the Indians; and children like those from Church On The Rock, Nederland, Texas, who sent boxes of toys to the poor in Mexico and Cuba—all of these not only believe that we can build a bridge, but they are helping to build that bridge.

The apostle Paul said, "Now abides three, faith, hope and love, and the greatest of the three is love"; and love can build a bridge.

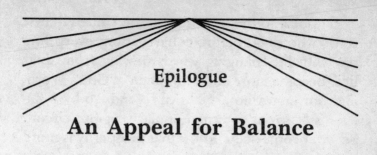

Epilogue

An Appeal for Balance

I wrote this book with two goals in mind: first to recount something of my journey, to tell something of my story; secondly, to encourage others to take up their own journeys and by God's grace accomplish their purpose in life. There is only one further matter I hope to communicate, and it is an appeal for balance in the life of the Church.

I appeal to all the denominations to recognize the importance of other groups in completing the work of the Kingdom of God. We are all part of the body of Christ, and we all need each other. Think of the great victories to be won when we work hand in hand for the common cause of Christ's gospel. May God forgive us for our competitive spirits and cause us to compete with the powers of darkness and not with one another.

I appeal to religious organizations to recognize the sovereign hand of God and give Him the freedom to change human policies when He needs to. Rules are necessary, but man's judgments are not always God's. There are always exceptions to the rules we make.

I appeal to the ministers in the United States: those who stand before congregations every Sunday with life-changing words flowing from their lips. Become more and more men of God's Word, and not men who are blown to and fro by whatever is "current" on the popular religious circuit. Set your roots deep. Know that prosperity is more than material gain. Preach the whole of God's Word and not upper-class American values. God is building His kingdom, and He is making its foundations sure. May we be built upon the solid Rock of its Truth, and not our own ingenuities.

Finally, I appeal to you all to remember the poor. When Paul was accepted by the apostles in Jerusalem, they had one request of him: "All they asked was that we should continue to remember the poor, the very thing I was eager to do" (Gal. 2:10). The ultimate question of our wealth is not whether we have had faith enough to accumulate it, but whether we have had heart enough to share it.

I join with the apostles and appeal to you: remember the poor.